T0292861

China In
Transition

10 Case Studies on Chinese Companies

Breaking the Mold

China In Transition

By CKGSB Case Center

ISBN-13: 978-988-8552-42-9

BUSINESS & ECONOMICS

EB122

Published by Earnshaw Books Ltd. (Hong Kong)

CONTENTS

Acknowledgements

This book is based on the research and original insights of the CKGSB professors and researchers, who are mentioned in the case studies hereafter. We are thankful for their wise input shared during the research and initial writing of these case studies. We are also grateful to Professor Li Wei and Assistant Dean Zhou Li for their recognition of this work.

We would like to express our gratitude to Heather Mowbray, whose edits shaped this book, and to Graham Earnshaw at SinoMedia for his support throughout.

Finally, we thank our colleagues from the CKGSB Case Center—in particular, Yang Yan and Mei Xinlei—and the Global Marketing and Communications team—Ira Zaka, Jessica Wang and Tian Xuefang. This book would not have been possible without their dedication, thorough efforts and expertise.

Foreword

Private Enterprise as a Role Model

Zhou Li, Assistant Dean, CKGSB

Over the past four decades, the one constant factor in the development of China's economy and society has been "change," on a scale rarely seen in human history. Today, China is transitioning into an era of even more profound change, stimulated by its fast growing and increasingly competitive consumer market, its well-educated workforce and its dazzling speed of adopting and developing new technologies.

New technologies, whether Internet or AI-based, are creating new opportunities and giving rise to new business models. Innovation in finance is encouraging technology companies to re-list on China's A-share markets, a trend which reflects the extent to which the capital markets now embrace the innovation-led new economy. Technological developments have helped with small and medium-sized enterprise financing, particularly in rural areas, injecting vitality into a sector of the economy that traditional banking could not service.

Social issues such as income inequality, education and the traditional public welfare model are increasingly under the spotlight. New innovative and philanthropic solutions are in urgent need. To understand China today, it is essential to understand this sector and its innovative force.

Private enterprises, such as those discussed in this book, are pioneers providing the spark which ignites the economic, technological and social change as well as the vitality essential for progress. As China's reform agenda reaches deeper, less predictable waters, the adaptability of these companies will be essential to steering a safe course.

In the past 16 years, the Cheung Kong Graduate School of Business, with the most influential business people in the private sector numbered amongst its student body, has been an active participant in China's economic transition and has had the opportunity to observe maturing private enterprises from close up, and to play a role in educating them. This selection of recent case studies from CKGSB's Case Study Center examines the concepts and principles of companies that are driving China's growth and, in turn, changing the way business is done around the world. These studies provide a corporate viewpoint on what is happening in China's economy now and an outlook as to what will happen next.

Every shift in thinking generates a new type of economic vitality and social progress. 40 years ago, this was manifested in a group of entrepreneurs who were prepared to "cross the river by feeling the stones" – to be adaptable and innovative as they explored the unknown. They were well rewarded for their courage, as was China.

Today, we face another defining moment, a deepening of the reform process which places a higher requirement on the entrepreneurial spirit of China's private enterprises as well as the state-owned-enterprises (SOEs), multinational corporations (MNCs) and even the non-governmental organizations (NGOs).

In this new era, we need to emphasize the shaping of China's new business culture and encourage a return to "humanistic values." Entrepreneurs will be motivated to innovate not just by their own interests, but also by their ideals and dreams, and their sense of global responsibility.

Foreword

The Spark That Drives Transformation

Li Wei, Professor of Economics, Director of the Case Center and Director of the China Economy and Sustainable Development Center at CKGSB

For decades, business students in China have spent many hours in class discussing the best business practices embodied in case studies of iconic Western companies, distilling from these cases concepts and models that may be relevant for Chinese managers and entrepreneurs, all with the strong subtext that Chinese companies have much to learn from elsewhere. That is still true to an extent, and will likely remain so for years to come. But in recent years, the rest of the world has increasingly taken a strong interest in finding out more about how the best business practices by China's home grown champions may serve as relevant examples to follow.

The CKGSB Case Center hereby presents a collection of 10 case studies of Chinese businesses, examining how they are, in their different ways, embracing change and creating new business models for the future. They may not all be success stories, but they each, in different ways, reflect the ambition, innovation and pragmatism that are required to thrive in the hyper-competitive Chinese business environment.

Several case studies focus on on the role of mergers and acquisitions (M&A) for traditional companies to upgrade technological capabilities, to adopt new business models and to expand into new markets. Household appliance giant Midea's controversial takeover of the German robotics firm KUKA is examined in terms of the deal's impact on both companies and its suitability as a model for other companies aiming to achieve a similar transformation. Another chapter reviews the efforts of China's telecommunications giant Huawei to acquire US companies in order to restructure and expand its business.

But M&A is not the only path to corporate transformation. The spark of change often come from within, as seen with white goods manufacturer Haier and garment retailer HLA, two companies whose CEOs risked all in their embrace of the new. With Haier, it was the integration of new technologies, particularly internet technologies, into the company's business model, while HLA bet on a new business model to subvert traditional practices. The changes not only provided the firms with a path to survival and growth, but also a roadmap for companies elsewhere that are looking to adapt to the increasingly interconnected economy.

Then there is the trend of "mass entrepreneurship and innovation" – startups that are adapting and localizing ideas for China, while innovating beyond the original concept to create something better suited to the new business ecosystem. We look at how Ucommune is taking the shared office space model made famous by WeWork and developing it in the context of China's special circumstances, and how Tujia, a company inspired by Airbnb, has adapted the shared accommodation model. Hema Fresh, meanwhile, is remaking the whole concept of selling fresh food through a unique online-and-offline model that is less about localization and more about innovation.

Financial markets and institutions have played important roles in China's economic development. Qihoo 360, a security software company backed by several domestic and global venture capital firms, went public on NYSE in 2011, was taken private in 2016 and then re-listed on Shanghai Stock Exchange in 2018, all aided by strong support for technology firms by financial institutions and markets both in the US and in China. The relative underdevelopment of Chinese financial institutions have given many shadow banks opportunities to grow rapidly. One particular success story is Ant Financial, a financial technology company split off from Alibaba, one of China's technology giants. Ant Financial has used internet technologies and big data to redefine micro financing and open up new opportunities for businesses in parts of the Chinese economy that have been underserved by traditional banks: small and rural businesses.

For the last case, we turn to the Adream Foundation, a charitable foundation which has developed a new approach to charity and education in China by integrating business and financial management models in their operations.

In short, we selected these cases to help throw light on how some of China's most vibrant private businesses are re-making themselves and thereby contributing to the transformation of the Chinese economy. For fellow Chinese business people and also for managers and entrepreneurs in other parts of the world, we believe that these cases may well contain ideas worth exploring, pondering and perhaps debating.

Case Studies

1. Adream Foundation

Applying Business Logic to Philanthropy

Supervising Professor: Zhu Rui; Case Researchers: Cui Huanping, Zhu Yunhai

It may not have been the goal of Adream Foundation's founders, Pan Jiangxue and Wu Chong, to rework the philanthropic relationship between its donors and recipients, but that is what they ended up doing. While their concrete aim was to improve educational quality in China's countryside and inner cities, it was perhaps inevitable that these two financiers would attempt to inject a dose of efficiency that was sorely missing in China's charity sector in 2007. Adream found a way to make a mark, not just by scaling up nationwide efforts towards an admirable cause, but also by repositioning philanthropy as a successful and trustworthy financial proposition in a developing country full of civic potholes. They inherited a linear charity model and invented an integrated resource platform, turning schools, teachers, local governments, and donors into impassioned "dream partners."

Structured like a business and operated on commercial lines, Adream is powered by the language of efficiency, and the use of business matrixes and financial models. And just like a company, it offers a range of products. These include custom-designed classrooms known as "Adream Centers," lesson plans that form the "Adream Curriculum," a training program for teachers called the "Adream Guide," and "Adream Box," an online support platform for teachers. In the ten years since its founding in 2007, the foundation has set up 2,973 Adream Centers spanning the length and breadth of China, serving three million plus students and teachers in every province and region.

How Adream started

Before founding Adream, founders Pan Jiangxue and Wu Chong both served as senior executives in finance. In 2007, they each resigned from their respective posts, with the aim of establishing a charity based on their core belief: that educational quality was more important than educational hardware. They felt it important to enhance the student learning experience, upgrade their knowledge, abilities and attitudes, and look beyond the school gates to future prospects for China's children. With these goals in mind, the "Adream team" set about devising a charity that focused on "competency-based" education.

In practice, this was anything but straightforward. In October 2007, Pan and Wu incorporated the Cherished Dream China Education Fund in Hong Kong. They began working with the Shanghai office of Project Hope, a state-backed public service organization, but the two organizations were mismatched. Project Hope's Shanghai office provided funds to local foundations to set up Hope schools – staying away from construction and operations themselves. The model favored by Pan and Wu involved close monitoring of how the money was spent and heavy involvement in project operations.

In 2008, the fund tried to register as a private charitable foundation in mainland China, and hit a major snag. Registration was a complicated process, and they were having difficulty tracking down the right people to process their application. On May 12, 2008, all this changed. News came in of a devastating earthquake in the mountains of Sichuan province. The Wenchuan earthquake killed more than 87,000 people and devastated cities, roads, and schools. Within a week, Adream had delivered more than 10,000 tents to the disaster area, accounting for 3.67% of the national total, displaying an efficiency that shocked the Shanghai Bureau of Civil Administration. Soon after, the fund was classified as a "special talent" NGO, and on August 14, 2008, received its all-important registration, undersigned by six founding sponsors[1].

The newly-approved Adream Foundation had three guiding principles:

1. Helping people help themselves – assisting those who are motivated to improve and determined to change.

---

[1]   Pan Jiangxue, Wu Chong, Wang Jiyi, Yang Wei, Liu Man, and Shi Junming.

2. Using management and financial models, and making charity a form of social investment and a way to participate in social governance.
3. Building professional, effective, and sustainable charitable operations, and providing charity workers with meaningful careers.

Building a standardized process

Having set their sights on providing quality education to marginalized parts of China, the Adreamers turned their attention to the "products" they planned to offer. They had originally wanted to set up libraries, but on investigation found that remote libraries were hardly being used. Classrooms on the other hand were in strong demand, so to maximize their value proposition, centers equipped with the Internet, computers, books, and multimedia devices were selected as the basic units of Adream's quality education plan.

These first Adream Centers proved hard to set up in remote areas. At first, the Foundation sent designers to each site to map out and design each center individually, with the mission of creating places children could broaden their horizons in a modern and vibrant setting. The centers were then constructed with the help of local education bureaus. But soon problems including bidding irregularities and problems with delivery of customized furniture to mountaintop villages made them think again.

In 2010, a far more effective construction process was set in motion. From then on, Centers would have a standardized design and construction, and installation would be tendered out. School leaders need only download an online application form, and provide a floor plan and photographs from three specified angles, for the system to generate procurement lists according to a standard template. The central logistics system transports ready-to-assemble furniture to the school and the school finds a construction team at their own expense to assemble everything using Adream Foundation's construction manual. Teachers and students all get involved, and the Foundation only rarely has to step in to chase suppliers.

Standardization of the procedures has created operational efficiency, cost optimization and an economy of scale. From 2007 to 2016, the average construction period for an Adream Center fell from 180 days to 27 days. The speediest set-up was completed in one week. Costs were cut from RMB 110,000 to RMB 57,000 per center, and by 2016, a massive 448 centers could be built every year. In 2007, the number had been only two.

Figure 1: Annual Growth of Adream Centers

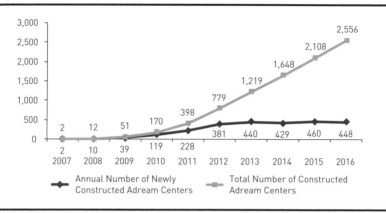

Source: Adream Foundation Annual Report

Starting in 2009, Adream partnered with third parties to develop its curriculum. Adream collaborated with East China Normal University's Institute of Curriculum and Instruction to develop the Adream Thirty, and with the Hong Kong Jockey Club to design its Youth Enhancement Scheme. Together with the University of Munich, it developed the Green Warrior program. Working with a number of financial institutions, it launched a range of Wealth Management courses.

The Adream Curriculum now comprises of 40 courses in three goal-oriented modules: "Who Am I?," "Where Am I Going?" and "How Do I Get There?" These are split into three grade levels: grades 1-3, grades 4-6, and grades 7-9. The "Who Am I?" module aims to develop students' self-awareness and recognition of their role in society and the environment; the "Where Am I Going?" module aims to encourage open-mindedness and creative thinking; and the "How Do I Get There?" module develops skills such as teamwork and problem-solving, and includes practical topics such as personal finance and career planning.[2]

The curriculum focuses on developing students' knowledge structures and thinking patterns, and fostering perspective, tolerance and innovation, so they can better face challenges with confidence. The courses can be replicated at every Adream Center. But while replicating the "knowledge product" itself may be easy, guaranteeing a high standard of instruction is

---

2   Introduction on Adream's official website.

harder. In devising the curriculum, Adream Foundation quickly found itself in need of a new product: teacher training. The Adream Guide followed soon after. And as the Foundation has found in setting up its Adream Centers, leaders at all levels needed to be on board. This led to the launch of the Adream Leader Project so that teachers, principals and local education directors could jointly create a sense of career purpose and a shift in values.

By 2010, the Adream Curriculum had been significantly upgraded, but teachers were still not giving over enough time to teaching Adream courses. To increase teacher engagement, a points-based incentive system was adopted. Teachers could submit reports on the Adream Curriculum and reflections on teaching it to an Adream Bank and earn credits based on the number of classes they held and the quality of course materials. National rankings were made public, with accumulated credits exchangeable for cash, training, travel and other rewards.

To provide social incentives for teachers too, the Adream Foundation developed Adream Box in March 2012. Teachers can post pictures of their classes, as well as upload and download course materials. The platform also let teachers contact others for advice and assistance in teaching particular courses. The more active teachers are on the platform, the more points they accumulate. In this way, hundreds of classes across the country can be monitored on a daily basis and course data can be collected and analyzed by a team of only four people. The Adream Box gets regular upgrades, and since 2015, has become a mobile platform, making operations faster and more convenient, and increasing community bonding.

With its four mutually supportive products – Adream Centers, Adream Curriculum, Adream Guide, and Adream Box – the Foundation had a package it could roll out in every school. In April 2017, the charity was certified by Lloyd's Register of Shipping and became the first foundation in China to pass ISO certification from an international organization. This proved that Adream had established an effective quality management system, and could guarantee quality services.

With a network of nearly 3,000 schools and partnerships with 600 education bureaus nationwide, Adream had succeeded in scaling up, thereby cutting the costs of replication and making the project more attractive to large donors.

Creating partnerships for change

Initially, the selection of Adream Center sites was a linear process. Donors would designate a region they wished to contribute to, Adream Foundation would ask the local education bureau to recommend a school and Adream would work with the school's principal to get the center established. At no stage was there any real screening or evaluation process. The charity decided to see what would happen if they made this an "organization-to-organization" model. Would it result in a big efficiency leap?

Today, education bureaus make a long list of the schools in their localities most in need of support. Adream Foundation evaluates them in terms of facilities, teaching philosophy, and willingness to dedicate time to the Adream Curriculum. The evaluation team ensures that selected schools have open-minded principals who get the concept, and the facilities to get the project off the ground. The original approach involved lengthy individual site visits; now sites are selected in standardized annual rounds. Adream Foundation has more time to promote its curriculum to local education bureaus, conduct risk assessment, and confirm best-fit recipients.

Promoting the Adream concept is an important step. Under standards implemented in 2001, each school has a 10% quota of the school week set aside for a local or school-based curriculum. This is the equivalent of three class periods. The aim had been to encourage schools to conduct more comprehensive studies, but in practice much of the time was swamped with more math and even more Chinese language, as these subjects were crucial for the all-important tests students would have to take later. Adream saw this slot in the curriculum as an opportunity and, from 2012, lobbied the authorities and education bureaus.

Adream Foundation then turned its attention to its main source of donations: companies. For partnerships to work, donor companies needed to participate fully. "We want the companies we cooperate with to identify with our philosophy and be able to promote Adream Centers in a sustainable way, rather than just pick donation targets according to poverty indices," said Hu Bin, Adream Foundation board director and former secretary-general. They also had to be ready to commit. "We need each donation to cover the construction of five to ten Adream Centers to reach economies of scale."

The charity also had to become more flexible about the funding models it would welcome. In addition to the direct funding model, some Adream Centers have been jointly funded by education bureaus and schools, and some by just the schools alone, with Adream coming in to provide follow-up services. In 2016, of RMB 94.75 million raised by Adream, government contributions accounted for as much as 24%.

Adream has transformed its charity recipients into partners, moving from the independent provision of products to the operation of a series of products and a community of users. This move towards community thinking is reflected not only in its cooperation with local governments, but also in its work with another key group of recipients – the teachers.

The foundation was growing so fast, it could not keep up with teacher and staff training, and costs were rising. So in 2011 Adream trialed a "Teachers' Salon" managed by teachers themselves, with education bureaus acting as consultants and the Foundation bearing daily operating expenses. The salon allows teachers to share materials and experiences, and encourages non-participating schools to learn more. By the end of 2016, there were 184 salons in up to 40% of all Adream schools, training nearly half of all "seed teachers"[3] in the system. Schools involved in a salon spent more class hours teaching more Adream courses than average. Today, this mutual support approach to teaching has been taken further. Adream Box has more than 30,000 users, for which it needs only one operator. Recipients, donors and volunteers are encouraged to help run the platform.

Adream Foundation is no longer a one-way supply channel. It has become a resource integration platform and a decentralized ecosystem, allowing education bureaus, schools, teachers, donors, and volunteers to become "Dream Partners" and work together to offer competency-based schooling.

Business innovation grounded in corporate governance

"Adream is driven by a strong sense of mission and values, and we operate in a professional way that revolves around the value of quality education," said co-founder Wu Chong. "As a result, we have formed a governance structure similar to that of an enterprise, using corporate vision and tools to resolve allocation problems in the face of limited resources and unlimited demand," he continued.

---

3   A "seed teacher" is a teacher who has completed one or more semesters as an Adream Curriculum instructor. After applying and being approved by the Foundation, a teacher can participate in "seed" teacher training, and have the opportunity to participate in Adream Curriculum demonstration classes or other sharing activities.

At Adream Foundation, a Board of Trustees sets strategic objectives, establishes policy and makes investment decisions. The chairman and the secretary-general direct the Secretariat to execute day-to-day managerial decisions. The Secretariat reports to the Board of Trustees, and the secretary-general, vice secretary-general and vice president report to the chairman of the board.

Co-founder Pan Jiangxue took her place on the Board of Trustees as chairman, alongside Wu Chong and four other senior executives from different industries.[4] One of their first actions was to set up three committees, for Strategy, Fundraising, and Audit & Compliance. As Pan Jiangxue said, "Only open, transparent, professional and efficient operations can secure the trust and sustained support of donors and the public. This is the same as the fiduciary duties of financial institutions."

The Foundation developed a functional organizational structure to support Adream Centers, curriculum development, teacher training, and post-maintenance. This consisted of an Adream Development Center,

Figure 2: Adream Foundation's Organizational Structure

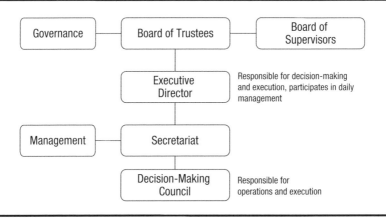

Source: Adream Foundation

---

4   Yang Wei, former vice president, Henan Pinggao Electric Company; Liu Man, executive director, Sales & Trading Department, China International Capital Company; Wang Jifei, chairman, Beijing Property & Credit Guarantee Company, and Shi Junming, partner, Shanghai Office of Dacheng Law Offices.

Operations teams[5], Fundraising teams[6], Branding and Communication Department, IT Department, Human Resources Department, Finance Department, Management Department and Office of the Director General.

Adream set up a multi-level authorization process, with clearly defined levels and periods of authorization. Proposals are submitted by the management team for the Board's approval. In practice, most proposals are implemented only if there has been a unanimous vote in their favor.

Adream Foundation has decentralized project implementation. Taking Adream Center site selection as an example, written evauations and telephone interviews with school principals are carried out by the Development Center, and a cross-departmental Risk Management Committee votes on every proposal. The chairman has veto power, but no right to raise a proposal.

As the number of Adream Centers swelled, a number of problems with Adream's management and operations emerged. Now with more than 80 staff, Adream had to find a sustainable way to pay workers enough to maintain standards. Pan Jiangxue believes that the availability of high quality staff is the main restriction on the Foundation's growth and quest for operational excellence. To keep a staff of high-quality employees, it has had to diversify its sources of funding for administration.

The Foundation's governing principles require that annual management costs must not exceed 10% of that year's total spending. But unlike many other foundations that just draw the 10% they need from donations, all Adream's administrative costs are covered by its administrative reserves, which consist of founding capital, donations designated for administrative purposes, unrestricted donations, and income from investments.

In order to reduce the staff salary burden, the Foundation separated out the Business Development Department and Project Construction Department, which are in charge of Adream Center site selection and construction, setting up a separate unit – the Shanghai Adream Charity Development Center.

Corporate governance structures took shape as Adream developed, with ongoing adjustments along the way. At the end of 2013, Adream brought

---

5   Comprised of Curriculum Service Department, Teacher Development Academy, Curriculum R&D Institute
6   Comprised of Public Fundraising Department, Huodui Funding Platform, Special Fund Department, Cooperation and Development Department

branding, human resources and big data experts onto the Board.[7] The Board of Supervisors expanded and the Board of Trustees established three new committees – Human Resources & Remuneration, Investment Management, and Curriculum Evaluation & Teacher Development. In 2016, He Jin, a former senior project officer at the Ford Foundation[8] became a director. Adream Foundation's internal management and ISO quality certification were also put on the agenda. In 2017, Shen Yu, with years of experience in quality certification and management, was appointed as director and secretary-general. By then the Board of Trustees totaled nine members.

Adream Foundation's expansion challenges

In 2016, Adream failed to reach its annual funding target for the first time. The Board had set a target of RMB 103 million, but the Adream team raised

Figure 3: Investment Income and Administrative Expenses (10,000 RMB)

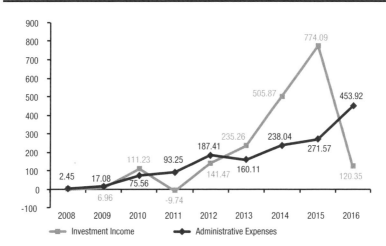

Source: Adream Foundation Annual Report

7   The newly-appointed directors included senior media professional Fang Xiangming and big data expert Tu Zipei; the new-appointed supervisors included Liu Yuan, CEO of Aon Hewitt (China) and a human resource expert, and also Cheng Jing, an expert in Internet Finance, Managing Director and CEO of Zhongan Online Insurance Company Inc.

8   Ph.D. from Stanford University, served with the United Nations and the World Bank.

Figure 4: Adream Organization Structure (2017)

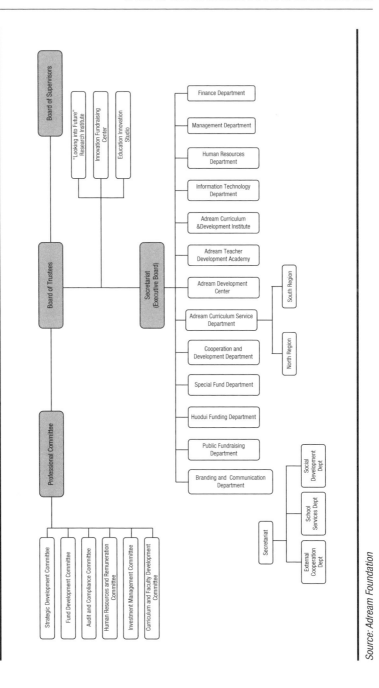

Source: Adream Foundation

just over RMB 94 million. The Foundation had to take a serious look at roadblocks to development, and unravel their connections to each other. The leadership team found that Adream faced three main issues, low brand awareness, unstable sources of funding, and unsustainable governance mechanisms.

Overcoming low brand awareness by developing public offerings

In order to improve branding awareness, in May 2011, Adream Foundation set up a fundraising department and started offering services for major donors. But in 2015, its functions were split into a Public Offerings Department and a Branding and Communications Department. The former was established to maximize Adream Foundation's online promotional capacities. As a relative latecomer to online branding and public offerings[9], Adream had to get to grips with phenomena such as microcharity,[10] which has become enormously popular in China. Grappling with how to use public charity platforms to launch crowdfunding campaigns, it established a platform on WeChat and worked with community organizations. In September 2015, an Internet startup program that Adream incubated – Huodui online public donation platform – was set up, and in less than two years, raised more than RMB ten million.

Securing funding sources, accelerating development of new channels

Adream uses four fundraising channels – governmental institutions, corporate donations, public fundraising platforms, and special funds – between which there is mutual support and a good balance. Its main fundraising issues have been threefold:

1. The largest portion of Adream's funding comes from high net-worth

---

9 The Public Offering Department came into being soon after Adream was granted public charitable foundation status in March 2014. This official status enabled Adream to spread its vision and influence online.

10 A charity participation mode based on SNS that is initiated by ordinary individuals and organizations to realize specific charity needs through extensive charitable participation. Sourced from "Influences of Altruistic Motivation, Shared Vision, and Perceived Accessibility on Microcharity Behavior," By Du, Lanying; Qian, Ling; Feng, Yi.

individuals and corporations. However, these two types of donors can be "picky." Corporations in China suffer from "donor fatigue," and no longer donate as much as they did. Regular donors may no longer be satisfied with a single charitable product. The Foundation is not sufficiently sensitive to changes in the charity landscape, with innovations not keeping apace with donor needs.

2. Adream's public fundraising efforts have lagged behind its peers in absolute terms. Because Adream started late in online public offerings and has limited funding reserves, its public offerings rely heavily on the Tencent platform and its 99 Public Welfare Day[11]. Adream had limited contact with other platforms and online channels.

3. Unrestricted donations[12] in support of Adream's long-term development have dropped off. 2016 was the first time that Adream was forced to use its administrative reserves, and the first year in which its reserves received no new funding injections.

Knowing full well that Rome was not built in a day, Adream Foundation undertook several measures.

It sought to improve the donor experience and secure more private placements. In the early days, Adream acted like an agency to its charity recipients. Donors used the Adream platform to make their contributions, and Adream reported back on the use of their funds. As Adream Centers proliferated, this kind of direct donor-recipient relationship became harder to sustain. "In the past, it was about assisting donors to serve the beneficiaries, but the donors did not have the chance to go deep into the donation areas and to see the impact of their support," Wu Chong said. "In the future, we will connect donors and schools (beneficiaries), strengthen donors' sense of participation and achieve fundraising sustainability."

It went about this by building a matrix of virtual teams in a newly spun off Cooperation and Development Department. It was subdivided into three regional entities which were responsible for keeping in touch with donors in their respective localities. Each virtual team comprised of an investment relations manager, a site selection manager and an operations manager, with

---

11 A fundraising program jointly launched by Tencent Public Welfare and hundreds of public welfare organizations, famous enterprises, celebrities, and innovation and marketing organizations on September 9 each year.

12 Unrestricted donations mean the donor has not made any requests as to the purpose prior to donating. Restricted donation means that the donor has requested that their donation be used for a special purpose. Restricted donations are divided into purpose-restricted donations and time-restricted donations.

a team leader coming from a different department and a regional manager reporting to headquarters. In this way, connections were strengthened with donors on site, and more private placements became feasible.

Soon after China enacted its Charity Law in March 2016, Adream Foundation became a trustee of the first new charitable trust in China. A year later, Adream launched the 2017 SDIC Adream No.2 Charitable Education Trust, China's first equity charitable trust. Until the new law came into being, many donors were restricted in the ways they could give, and wary of infringing the law. They tended to give to just large charities such as the Red Cross. Under the new law, trusts are legally permitted to work in the public interest and can fundraise more openly, and the new legal framework gave Adream the confidence to set up A-mazing Lab to look into creative solutions to fundraising dilemmas. These have so far included options such as establishing a sole trustee charitable trust or a charitable art trust.

Separating governance and management

Pan Jiangxue believes that Adream Foundation's efficiency and successful development can be put down to integrated decision-making and execution, woven into its governance structure. On the other hand, such a structure tends to involve over-reliance on the self-discipline, work ethic, dedication, and wisdom of the founders. Since this is not necessarily healthy for sustainable development, Pan Jiangxue has addressed this by tweaking the organization's corporate governance mechanisms. The division of authority between trustees and the secretary-general has been changed, so that executive managerial responsibilities can be better distributed.

The new mechanism means that day-to-day management at the Secretariat level is based on the outcome of votes by the Board of Trustees on cross-sectorial issues. Directors can submit proposals and make statements to promote them on a regular basis. The voting mechanism allows two votes for the proposer and one vote for each of the other directors, with a 2/3 majority required for approval. Pan Jiangxue, as executive director, has one veto vote.

Adream Foundation's impact

The Foundation set out to run a transparent charitable organization, an ambitious yet timely idea in a country where the level of trust in civil society organizations was low. It has become the first charity in China to publish annual reports using the same transparency standards as publicly-traded companies. From 2011 to 2014, Adream was annually hailed as "China's Most Transparent Charitable Foundation" by Forbes China. In 2016, Jiemian News, a Shanghai-based new media platform, came to the same conclusion.

Adream has attempted to implement quality education offerings across China using an operational model that was borrowed from the business world. The charity raised a total of RMB 570 million between 2008 and 2017. It built 2,973 Adream classrooms, and brought more than three million teachers and students in under its umbrella. What impact has its operational model had on this success? And what influence has competency-based education had on students and teachers in the system? How does Adream go about adjusting its product offerings to better meet the needs of its end users, children in rural China?

Like a business, Adream has developed internal appraisal standards that measure two sets of KPIs: those followed by each department, and those developed to evaluate the virtual teams operating across China. The latter are evaluated by fundraising targets, class opening rates and student attendance.

In November 2013, Adream launched the Adream Center evaluation project and hired a team of assessors from the Center for Chinese Agricultural Policy, Chinese Academy of Sciences, Center for Chinese Agricultural Policy, Peking University, Center for Experimental Economics in Education, Shaanxi Normal University, and the Rural Education Action Plan (REAP)[13] team from Stanford University to conduct a third-party independent report into the impact of Adream Centers on students and teachers. The team selected 166 primary, junior high and comprehensive schools from 13 districts and counties of Shanxi, Shaanxi, Hubei, Guizhou, and Fujian. Among these, 85 were participant schools and 81 were selected as a control group. The assessment team also conducted a three-year follow-up survey.

The results showed that Adream Courses have had a positive impact in the following ways: First, Adream participants have scored higher than those in the control group schools. Second, attitudes towards the function and value of money were found to have improved due to participation in Adream

---

13 An impact evaluation organization that aims to inform sound education, health and nutrition policy in China. REAP's goal is to help students from vulnerable communities in China enhance their human capital and overcome obstacles to education so that they can escape poverty and better contribute to China's developing economy." Sourced from official REAP website.

Wealth Management courses, through which students learned and practiced personal financing. There was also a significant improvement in attitudes with regard to the role and value placed on rights. The Adream Curriculum and life skills learned during the courses have allowed the students to experience the function of rights and change their way of thinking about them.

Adream Foundation has decided on its next round of improvements based upon the evaluation team's findings. First, to upgrade Adream Center equipment, giving all participants Internet access and the use of tablet computers. This will also provide Adream with more daily data. Second, to establish an online management system with teachers as contact persons and students as recipients of assistance, allowing for real-time tracking and evaluation. Third, to train teachers in process management. For example, before, during and after each course, teachers will test the students and upload files, so that the teachers can clearly understand the tasks to be undertaken and effectively allocate their time and energy.

The Adream Center Impact Assessment project has provided an objective perspective on the charity's implementation of competency-based education in rural areas of China from a third-party perspective. The evaluation results indicate that the Adream Foundation's integration of managerial and operational models from the business world has helped in their implementation of quality education in hard-to-reach parts of the country.

This study of Adream's journey has shown how, despite its enormous successes and praise-worthy expansion, the Foundation has been hampered by various shortcomings and external challenges. As a pioneer, this is perhaps inevitable. Importantly, though, Adream Foundation is well aware of its issues, and is actively seeking solutions to them in line with the vision of its founders using its increasingly responsive and evolving corporate governance system.

2. Hema Fresh

Alibaba's New Retail Business

Supervising Professor: Jing Bing; Case Researcher: Li Mengjun

Linda is an executive who works long hours. Her husband also often gets home late. Both find themselves too tired to answer the children's caretaker when she asks, "What would you like to eat tomorrow?" One night, Linda came across an app on her phone for Hema Fresh. She downloaded it and now, sometimes long after midnight, she can select fresh produce for next-day delivery. With its seasonal suggestions and cooking tips, Linda feels grateful to Hema for knowing that her family will eat well. She has become a major fan.

Regardless of whether an e-commerce fresh produce supplier choses a B2C model or an O2O one, whether an agent who buys at the wet market or a traditional store delivery service, each one is trying to resolve the same kind of household consumer issue. When put to the test, these models sink or swim on how effective they are, what kind of consumer experience they offer, and how sustainable they are commercially. And as Jack Ma, executive chairman of Alibaba Group, has said: "The era of pure e-commerce will soon be over, and in the next 20 to 30 years, there will be no e-commerce, only new retail."

Hema Fresh is a new Alibaba venture in the fast-moving consumer segment of fresh produce. It uses both an app and offline stores to offer its services. Offline stores deliver experiential services and the app provides quality takeaway options and fresh produce delivery. Hema Fresh only began in January 2016. By February 2018, the company had 30 stores in cities including Shanghai, Beijing, Shenzhen, Hangzhou, and Guiyang.

"The Hema Fresh store in Shanghai Jinqiao had an annual turnover of approximately RMB 250 million in 2016, averaging RMB 56,000 per unit area, much higher than the industry average of RMB 15,000. Hema Fresh's app conversion rate is as high as 35%," said Hema Fresh Founder Hou Yi.

With back-end digital and smart technical support, a successful closed-loop consumer model has been created. Although new, Hema Fresh's business model has been adopted by leading supermarket Yonghui with its "Super Species" as well as several other players.

Fresh food, retail and the competitive landscape

Due to the special characteristics of fresh food products, in 2016, online penetration was only 1.6%, far below that of clothing, cosmetics and mobile phones. China's first fresh food e-commerce vendor Yiguo Fresh was established in 2005, initiating a period of rapid development for the fresh food e-commerce market. In 2018, the market segment is forecast to be worth RMB 194.8 billion, an increase of 40% over the previous year.[1]

In the early stages, the fresh food e-commerce companies focused on online business and heavy capital input, choosing to build their own cold chain and logistics teams. High delivery costs forced companies to position their products in the medium and high-end of the market in an effort to subsidize logistics costs with higher-priced orders. But this market positioning also limited sales volume, making it difficult for operators to generate sufficient order quantity or density[2] while high delivery costs devoured their profits. That plus ineffective management of fresh food supply chains led to high product wastage rates and poor customer feedback, putting the companies at a disadvantage compared to bricks-and-mortar stores.

In August 2015, Fruitday adopted an online to offline (O2O) strategy using physical stores and a two-hour delivery service. However, offline operations were a burden in terms of store management, supply chain optimization and other aspects, and in 2016, Fruitday had to close almost all of its physical stores, because of poor site selection, unprofessional management and rising rental costs. Online operatives at Wal-Mart and Yonghui similarly gave up on efforts to develop their own "last mile" logistics. Tmall and JD.com have established jointly-operated O2O models in which fresh food products are

---

1   iResearch.
2   "Order density" refers to the number of orders in a given area. If the order density is high, then the logistics efficiency level is also higher.

Figure 1: Scale of Fresh Food Business in China

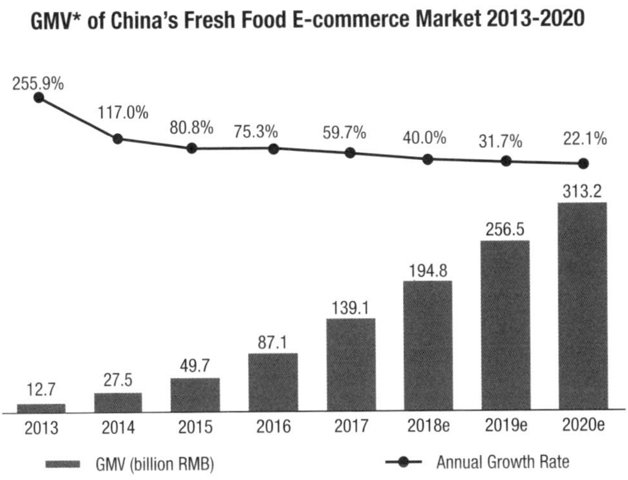

GMV* of China's Fresh Food E-commerce Market 2013-2020

Source: iResearch

selected from markets only on receipt of online orders.[3]

Yet according to the Research Institute on Prospective Industries, of China's more than 4,000 fresh food e-commerce companies, 7% are suffering big losses, 88% are slightly unprofitable, 4% break even and only 1% are profitable. The fresh food market is "dirty work," but because it is a solid and high-repurchase category with huge growth potential, Internet giants such as JD.com and Alibaba Group have become involved.

How Hema Fresh began

Before incubating Hema Fresh, Alibaba Group opened its own online fresh food store, Tmall Fresh, consisting of three major channels for different

---

3   Miao Tmall (天猫喵鲜生) targets high-end customers and imported fresh food, provides customers with one-stop shopping. JDHome (京东到家) integrate various O2O life categories, provide consumers with fresh foods and supermarket product distribution, and implement fast delivery within two hours based on LBS positioning.

*   The GMV of China's fresh food e-commerce market only includes GMV in the online channel of the companies with online and offline sales channels such as Fresh Hema. The data were calculated in accordance with the financial results of the related enterprises and interviews with experts in iResearch statistical model.

consumer groups – Tmall supermarket, Miao Tmall, and Tmall flagship stores. It then participated in four investment rounds of Yiguo Fresh[4] and built a cold chain logistics platform, Exfresh[5].

In November 2016, Alibaba bought a 32% stake in the bricks-and-mortar grocery chain Sanjiang[6], becoming its second-largest shareholder. In December of the same year, Yiguo Fresh invested in Lianhua[7], making it the Chinese supermarket chain operator's second-largest shareholder. In November 2017, Alibaba Group invested HK$22.4 billion to obtain a 36.16% stake in Sun Art Retail[8].

Hou Yi, founder and CEO of Hema Fresh, started out in logistics, and joined Alibaba Group's main rival in produce services, JD.com, becoming director of JD Home. In early 2015, he left JD to embark on a different route for the fresh food sector. Hou Yi believed retailers should expand offline stores and take advantage of mobile Internet technology. More physical stores meant faster development of brand awareness, lower customer acquisition costs, and lower cost for cold chain delivery. He wanted to create integrated online-offline supermarkets, restructuring the entire model.

Zhang Yong, CEO of Alibaba Group, entered into discussions with Hou Yi and in March 2015, launched Hema Fresh, with seven original founders. On January 15, 2016, the Shanghai Jinqiao store was opened and the Hema Fresh app was released.

Strategic positioning at Hema Fresh

Positioned as a boutique supermarket, Hema Fresh targets a younger consumer generation that seeks quality, is less cost-sensitive and more time-sensitive. Each online order has quite similar fulfillment costs (picking, packaging, and courier services), so relatively larger purchase orders are more cost-efficient. Strategically, Hema Fresh offers seafood at a lower price

---

4   In 2013, Alibaba made an exclusive investment on Yiguo Fresh of US$ ten million, and then participated in a B round investment together with Yunfeng Capital in 2014. In 2016, Yiguo Fresh finished its C round financing with Alibaba leading the round, and then accepted the C+ Round financing with Suning leading with US$200 million. In 2017, Yiguo Fresh received its D round financing from Ali.

5   Exfresh (安鲜达), a subsidiary of Yiguo Fesh, is a fresh food cold-chain distribution company, providing one-stop cold-chain warehouse services for customers in the fresh food industry.

6   Being the leader in Zhejiang chain retailers, Sanjiang (三江购物) has over 160 stores.

7   Lianhua Supermarket (联华超市) has 3,796 stores in eastern China, mainly neighborhood markets and convenience stores.

8   Sun Art Retail is a leading retailer with hypermarket and fast-growing E-commerce businesses in China.

than other channels, targeting middle and high-income young people. A complete range of seafood, from expensive Boston lobsters to king crabs is on display in stores, and products can be prepared and cooked on the spot. Hema Fresh's pricing strategy is to rely on seafood to attract customers and make profit from other categories. Hema Fresh outlets also sell fresh vegetables and meat, while snack foods and daily commodities account for a small proportion of its turnover.

Online/offline integration

Hema Fresh has adopted a business model of high integration of online and offline channels supported by Alibaba's big data system. It focuses mainly on online sales supplemented by offline sales. The physical stores serve as warehouses and distribution centers for online orders within a three-kilometer radius. The products sold online and offline are exactly the same, with the same quality and the same prices.

Offline supermarket operations – Store layout and product placement

The design of traffic flows within Hema Fresh supermarkets is different from other supermarkets, reflecting the concept of customer-oriented omni-channel operations. Hema Fresh differs from traditional supermarkets by providing multiple entrances and exits, and giving customers free access to stores. In terms of product placement, Hema's seafood products are usually placed at the main entrances and exits, or other conspicuous locations. There are different seafood promotions every day.

Taking Hema Fresh's Shilibao store in Beijing as an example, SKUs (Stock Keeping Units) number around 8,000. The quality of imported products is high, the packaging is good and prices are reasonable. Fruits and vegetables are already packed in boxes and bags, reducing weighing time and wastage. In addition to direct imports, there are also some jointly-marketed imported products (such as red wine). Dedicated staff handle the sorting of goods, and each has a mobile handheld terminal FDA capable of receiving goods, returning goods, managing inventory and packaging. A staff member said the so-called "micro-chain system" allows Hema Fresh to pick and pack items within ten minutes.

Table 1: Implications of Online/Offline Integration

	Features	Description
Online	Online business improves store efficiency and business performance	• According to data from Hema's Jinqiao Store, 4,000 online orders daily account for 50% of the total, and revenue per unit area is RMB 32,400 (excluding catering and other revenue), three times higher than traditional supermarkets • In terms of profit, average online transaction per customer is RMB 70 (US$10.20). After deducting 25% gross profit, delivery and packaging fees, it is basically still possible to achieve a net profit
	Online business builds up user systems and collects data and information	• Hema can only accept payment online using the Hema app, which helps to promote cash-free transactions and refines the user system through the app • Traditional supermarkets relying on cash payments are at a disadvantage with no way to independently extract and synergize payment data
Offline	Good offline user experience and premium quality feeling are an endorsement of online services	• New changes in Hema's offline arrangements enhance user convenience and experience • Structure of product offerings and quality of store decoration enhance the premium quality feeling • Excellent offline user experiences establish a brand effect and guide users from offline to online
	Offline stores serve as "front-line warehouses" to ensure on-time delivery	• Hema's commitment is to deliver within 30 minutes which, compared with same day or following-day delivery as offered by traditional e-commerce, is much more efficient • Hema has 5,000 SKUs (Stock Keeping Units), less than traditional supermarkets, which improves selection efficiency
	Stores serving as "front-line warehouses" to cut costs	• Supermarkets attract consumer traffic to shopping malls and can enjoy preferential rents. As "front-line warehouses", Hema stores serve as distribution centers, providing a significant reduction in rental costs • Traditional e-commerce distribution centers are usually located on the outskirts of cities mainly due to excessively high rental costs in city centers

Source: CKGSB Case Study Center

Online order delivery

The Hema Fresh app is currently used mostly for fresh food deliveries, but medium and high-end delivery services for other produce may be added in the future. With the e-commerce business sharing warehouse and distribution systems with the offline stores, storage costs are relatively low and delivery times from store to nearby customers are relatively short, making it possible to guarantee product freshness and on-time delivery within 30 minutes inside a three-kilometer radius.

Figure 2: Delivery Process of Hema Fresh's Online Orders

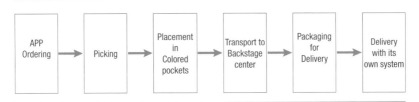

Source: CKGSB Case Center

It is worth noting that Hema Fresh has adopted a distributed order picking approach to raise efficiency. The algorithm breaks down an order and assigns each part to different pickers, instead of the traditional way in which one person picks all of the goods in an order. Three minutes maximum each is allocated for picking the items of an order, transferring bags to the delivery warehouse and packing the products. After nine minutes of processing, the fulfilled order "rides" the vertical lift system and 20 minutes is left for road delivery. The Shanghai Jinqiao store, for example, has around 100 couriers to ensure delivery is completed within 30 minutes. Hema Fresh has also built its own logistics system encompassing CRT (Controlled Room Temperature) logistics and cold chain logistics, as well as logistics distribution centers and temporary ponds for live seafood.

Procurement management

Hema has adopted a buyer model[9] for centralized purchasing, allowing for direct sourcing from around the world to bring consumers high-quality products at reasonable prices. Some of Hema's fresh food products are jointly procured with Tmall Fresh. All cherries and Boston lobsters available in-store are sourced in collaboration with Tmall Global. With other categories of products, such as products in the "daily fresh" program[10], Hema Fresh ensures product quality by forging partnerships with agricultural produce bases and also through "made-to-order" production and end-to-end cold chain arrangements. Hema also directly cooperates with providers such as Shanghai Bright Food Group, COFCO (China Oil & Foodstuffs Corporation) and other large food groups to ensure product quality. At the same time, it also sets prices at the lowest level in the industry.

Big data and technical back-end support

Hema Fresh has upgraded its service experience with a mandatory mobile payment method and efficient delivery system by adopting "IoT (Internet of Things)" technology. The company relies on big data support from Alibaba Group, especially in R&D, voice computing capabilities, and distribution algorithms. Using big data, consumer profiles are more accurate, helping the company establish precision marketing campaigns and well-chosen stores.

To optimize data capture, Alibaba Group's online payment system, Alipay, is encouraged as the main payment method. Hema Fresh has also connected with Taobao.com and the Alipay membership system for data and ecosystem sharing. Customers can directly pay by scanning QR codes, with the data uploaded to the analysis platform via Alipay and the Hema Fresh app. After processing and analysis, this data is passed back to Hema Fresh and Alipay for commercial use.

---

9   Professional procurers are responsible for sourcing and hand-picking the right goods to sell.
10 Meat, vegetables, and dairy products are brought in and replaced each day to ensure that only the freshest items are available.

Figure 3: Hema's Back-end Technical Support

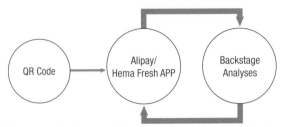

QR Code scanning helps establish an IoT closed loop at the retail front-end

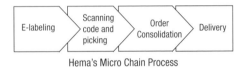

Hema's Micro Chain Process

Source: Industrial Securities Research

The Hema Fresh business logic

What is the underlying business logic of the Hema model? Hou Yi has said that, "All that Hema does may seem like the so-called omni-channel online-offline business model, but in essence it is the reconstruction of 'people, goods and marketplace,' it is a retail revolution creating new consumer values and leading to new ways of life."

Reshaping the relationship between "people, goods, and marketplace"

Changes to the "people" factor rely on Alibaba's big data, which allows Hema to analyze customers in a multi-dimensional way to help it meet their demands more precisely. For "goods," Hema is adopting direct sourcing, small-package design and a flexible settlement approach, putting itself more in line with consumer shopping habits. For the "marketplace" factor, from Hema Fresh to Hema Food Market and on to Hema F2 convenience stores, the consumer experience is constantly upgraded and customers are encouraged to form new consumer habits.

Restructuring the value chain

Hema Fresh has now completed its initial integration of online and offline channels and optimized its internal business processes. For retailers, channels are their most valuable resource. Hema Fresh's founder, Hou Yi, is not satisfied with the level of channel integration, and has repeatedly stressed that Hema's core competitiveness is to give consumers good products. He believes that, theoretically speaking, circulation losses within and between enterprises can be brought down to zero, reshaping the value chain. The future of the retail industry, he says, must be "in the hands of retailers."

For Hema Fresh, its next move is to launch its own branded products. In December 2017, it introduced "Hema-Anchor"[11] fresh milk, marking the first time that Hema has created a complete supply chain for its own brand. By doing so, it aims to reconfigure the supply chain, reduce costs through large-scale procurement, remove intermediate distribution channels, reduce marketing costs and change the pricing mechanism. By optimizing the supply chain, Hema Fresh can gain both bargaining power and pricing power, controlling both quality and cost.

Figure 4: "People, Goods and Marketplace" in New Retail

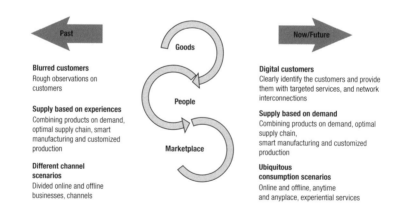

Source: CKGSB Case Center

11   A brand of fresh milk jointly launched by Hema and Anchor.

Figure 5: Restructuring the Value Chain

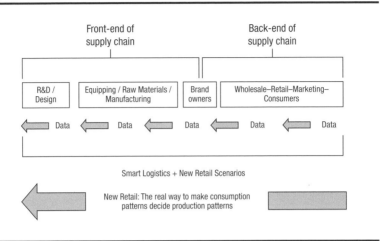

Source: Ali Research, Industrial Securities Research

New Retail in the e-commerce future

With the rise of e-commerce, as well as rising property and labour costs, traditional bricks-and-mortar retail businesses have experienced setbacks. But on the other hand, while e-commerce is popular in China, its growth has begun to level off and the online platforms alone are no longer a cheap and effective means of acquiring new customers. The New Retail model has appeared at a time when the performance of traditional retail stores looks bleak, and e-commerce is approaching a bottleneck.

In a speech in October 2016, Jack Ma raised the concept of "New Retail" for the first time, and created a storm in the retail sector.

Companies that rely on the Internet to upgrade and transform their production processes, distribution and sales channels through the use of big data or artificial intelligence can be called New Retail businesses. The business structure and ecosystem is reshaped, as a result, bridging e-commerce, physical retail and logistics in order to improve the efficiency of both selling and buying goods, as well as enhancing the shopping experience. Hema Fresh is an example of New Retail in practice, offering a new way of thinking about retail.

2017 was defined by Alibaba as being Year One of New Retail. Capital is always market-sensitive and the Internet tycoons have raced to implement their offline retail strategies, including Alibaba's investment in Sun Art Retail, and JD, and Tencent securing a holding in Yonghui Superstores[12]. New Retail is not so much a technological innovation as it is a change in the way of thinking. From the Hema Fresh case, we can see that New Retail, in essence, is a strategy that adapts to changes in customer demand by reconstructing value chains and commercial elements. The New Retail "war" is ultimately a competition over the nature of business.

Appendix

Fresh produce in Chinese retail

Food that is uncooked, unrefined or otherwise unprocessed presents a big challenge to the modern retail sector. Fresh food contains more SKUs (Stock Keeping Units), less standardization, shorter shelf life, higher wastage rates, tougher quality control issues and, most importantly, more stringent requirements in terms of preservation and transportation than other goods.

On the other hand, fresh food is the most consumed and most frequently bought category in daily life. What is more, the fresh food market is big. In 2016, the retail volume of fresh food in China totaled 324 million tons with retail sales of RMB 4.57 trillion, accounting for 13.8% of total social retail sales.[13] Fresh food has become the "Blue Ocean[14]" opportunity longed for by e-commerce giants and entrepreneurs. Even in 2016, when the capital markets saw a downturn, investments into the domestic fresh food e-commerce market amounted to RMB 6 billion.

The upstream sector of the fresh food industry chain is the production of fresh agricultural products. China's agricultural output ranks top in the world, but production is still dominated by smallholders and the concentration of production is low, making it hard to realize agricultural automation and enhance efficiency. The midstream sector of the chain is distribution, and the key pain points are the multiple levels into which distribution is divided and the high rate of product wastage. The downstream sector is retail. In terms

---

12 Yonghui Superstores is a China-based company, principally engaged in the operation of regular chain supermarkets
13 Euromonitor.
14 A marketing theory about creating new market space and ignoring the competition, developed by INSEAD professors W. Chan Kim and Renée Mauborgne in 2004.

of sales channels, sales of fresh food products in China are still dominated by farmers' markets, accounting for 73%, and supermarket channels, which account for 22%, much lower than in developed countries. Fresh food e-retailers account for only 3%.

Commercial food retail in China

In 1985, China abolished the controlled procurement and distribution system of the planned economy era, and the circulation of agricultural products began its transformation into a market system. As a result, farmers' markets started to develop, and they remain today the main channel for urban residents to buy fresh food.

Supermarkets began opening in the mid-1990s. After 1996, foreign capital flowed into the Chinese market and supermarket titans such as Carrefour, Wal-Mart, and Metro established their networks of stores and got into the fresh food business. The low prices and rich choices in these supermarkets as well as the provision of specialty products such as fresh foods won over the hearts of consumers. Meanwhile, individual and chain stores appeared all over China.

In 2002, to counter the perception of farmers' markets as "dirty, disorderly and inferior" and to address food security issues, China launched "the farmers' supermarket project.[15]" Since then, China has seen fast development of supermarkets with an annual growth rate as high as 70%.[16] As competition has intensified, fresh food has gradually become an important means for supermarkets to attract customers and improve their competitiveness. Supermarkets have therefore gradually improved their control over fresh food supply chains.

Fresh food supermarkets: Yonghui Superstores and Sun Art Retail

In 2010, China's fresh food market was valued at RMB 680 billion, and by 2016 had expanded to RMB 1.1 trillion, reflecting steady growth. Currently

---

15 The purpose of the project is to transform the farmers' markets into fresh food supermarkets, namely running fresh agricultural products using the supermarket model, so as to standardize products and services.

16 In 2000, retail transactions for all chain businesses accounted for no more than 6% of total wholesale and retail sales, but it was 25% in 2005.

the top five supermarkets in China are Sun Art Retail (8.3%), CR Vanguard (6.4%), Wal-Mart (5%), Carrefour (3.1%), and Yonghui Superstores (3%). In terms of revenues, net income and net income margins, Sun Art and Yonghui have both seen steady growth. Among the major supermarket operators, Yonghui's fresh food accounted for the highest share of income, reaching 45%, compared to Sun Art's 32%.

Yonghui Superstores have continued to grow over the past few years despite the overall downturn in the industry. In 2016, its operating income was RMB 49.2 billion with net income of RMB 1.24 billion from 560 stores across China. Yonghui's core competitiveness is its mature fresh foods supply chain, which extends to upstream agricultural regions. The company has established about 20 cultivation bases. Sun Art Retail is the largest and fastest-growing hypermarket operator in China. In 2016, Sun Art's retail sales revenue was RMB 100.4 billion, net profit was RMB 2.57 billion and it had 446 outlets. Sun Art initiated a fresh food direct sourcing project in 2015, and from 2016 launched a central kitchen project to produce and provide semi-processed products in test locations to improve the quality and stability of fresh foods.

The replacement of farmers' markets by supermarkets will continue, despite fresh food making higher demands on supermarkets in terms of capital requirements, internal operations and supply chain management, limiting their expansion potential.

3. Heilan Home

A Revolution in the Chinese Clothing Market

Supervising Professor: Li Lede; Case Researchers: Gu Chongqing, Li Chao

In late May 2017, chairman of Heilan Home (HLA), Zhou Jianping, was in a rush. He had just returned from Europe and was about to race off to Kuala Lumpur to open the company's first overseas store. This was just one of the many tasks on Zhou Jianping's to-do list, which included searching for suitable M&A targets, promoting the HLA brand overseas, incubating more womenswear and childrenswear brands to achieve a multi-brand strategy, preparing to build new Guangdong and Shanghai design centers, and strengthening HLA's e-commerce sales.

On Forbes China's richest 2017 list, HLA's 57-year-old founder Zhou Jianping was ranked the richest man in domestic fashion with a net worth of US$ 4.14 billion[1], and in 2016 HLA was ranked top in A-share garments with a market value of RMB 45.197 billion[2]. But Zhou Jianping was still not satisfied, and wanted HLA to become a Fashion Brand Management Platform encompassing a host of fashion brands each generating billions of yuan in annual sales.

From its origins as a small, local brand in a lower tier city to China's top menswear brand today, the rapid development of HLA can be attributed to it never seeing itself as an "independent" company, but rather as part of a

---

1 Forbes (2017). China's richest 2017: The full list of 400 billionaires. Retrieved November 1, 2018, from https://www.forbes.com/sites/russellflannery/2017/11/15/chinas-richest-2017-the-full-list-of-400-billionaires/#7cde1f32296b

2 Sohu (2017). 海澜之家老板周建平成时尚行业首富 [Heilan Home owner Zhou Jianping became the richest man in the fashion industry]. Retrieved November 1, 2018, from http://www.sohu.com/a/141148544_427022

brand value chain, striving to create a win-win business ecosystem, making full use of high-quality, low-cost social resources for growth.

Innovating a business model for a township enterprise

HLA used to be Xinqiao Third Woolen Mill in Jiangyin City, a township collective established in 1988.[3] After its restructuring in the 1990s and three upgrades from producing woolen wool to worsted wool to garments, HLA arrived at a crossroads. On the one hand, becoming a private brand retailer meant being squeezed by those who had once been its clients, but on the other, becoming an agent for other clothing brands meant being squeezed by supermarkets, shopping malls and other channels.

Zhou Jianping yearned to break out of this vicious circle. He visited major clothing chains in Japan in early 2002 and was impressed by the rich array of mid-range garments, and even more so by the self-service experience. He intuitively knew the fixed price, high quality, rich choice model had a strong competitive advantage and decided to bring it to China. On his return, Zhou immediately registered and established Jiangyin HLA Garment Co., Ltd. After further analysis of the market, he decided to position HLA in a market segment where the competition would be less fierce: affordable menswear of all categories and styles. Learning from his Japanese peers, he introduced the "one-stop shopping"[4] model for domestic menswear, opening up a "blue ocean" market within China's highly competitive clothing industry.

HLA's development has trekked a path of three stages since then: product sales, model transformation, and growing maturity. Through an innovative "chain-shop trusteeship" model, HLA has gradually developed an asset-light barbell structure (see Fig. 1). HLA focuses on brand marketing, supply chain management and store management, and strengthens coordination with suppliers and franchisees so that the three parties form a close-knit community of shared interests. The goal is to make the HLA brand value chain bigger and stronger, and to implement a positive operational model with all the industry chain links working tightly together, sharing risks and making a profit.

---

3   Heilan.com.cn (n.d). Major milestones. Retrieved November 1, 2018, from http://www.heilan.com.cn/en/approach.php?act=3

4   A one stop shop is a business or office where customers can get multiple service or all they need in one place.

Figure 1: HLA's "Asset-light Barbell" Business Model

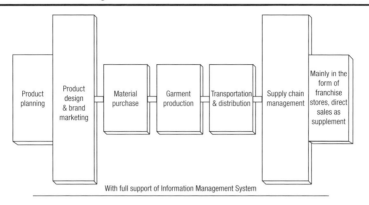

Source: CKGSB Case Center

Driven by this model, HLA has achieved rapid growth. The HLA brand was established in 2002 and the first store was opened in Nanjing[5] in September of that year. In 2004, HLA's annual retail sales exceeded RMB 100 million and in 2008 broke the 1 billion yuan mark. In 2009, HLA's first store in Tibet opened, and in 2010 its first store in Hainan[6], by which time HLA had stores across 31 provinces, autonomous regions and municipalities, covering more than 80% of China's counties and cities. The total number of stores nationwide reached 2,000 in 2011, close to 3,000 in 2013, nearly 4,000 in 2015, and by the end of 2016, totaled 5,243. Despite slower sales growth in China's clothing market and the resulting brick-and-mortar store closings, HLA had become an exception.

Today, with its "real man's closet" image, HLA offers a full range of menswear including suits, trousers, shirts, T-shirts, jackets. The high quality of its products, breadth of style, reasonable prices and personalized service has earned it broad popularity. Crease-resistant trousers, anti-static clothing, machine-washable suits and non-stretch T-shirts have become firm favorites, thanks to HLA's precise market positioning. HLA emphasizes low cost and rapid turnover, and prices its products at between half to one-third of the price of similar menswear brand products in China. For example, HLA's pure woolen suits range from RMB 380 to RMB 1,680 while on the market, they tend to cost between RMB 800 to RMB 3,000.

---

5   The capital of Jiangsu province.
6   The southernmost province of China mainland.

Apart from insisting on lower prices, HLA has put a lot of effort into improved product design since 2016, integrating fashionable elements into the formerly subdued and conservative business style. To attract a younger generation of consumers, it has launched several new product series including the "Fashion Jacket Series," "Colorful Denim Series," "Madagascar Range," "Famous Designer Cooperation Range" and "Fashion Overcoat Range."

Leveraging franchisees to achieve rapid expansion

The high-speed expansion of HLA is closely related to its store-opening approach. The three biggest international clothing brands – Uniqlo, H&M, and ZARA – use a direct-selling model which gives them full control over their sales channels, but limits their speed of expansion. Chinese menswear brands generally adopt a hierarchical agency system in which brand owners do not need to open their own stores, and instead use the sales channels of agents to achieve store number expansion within a short period of time. However, because franchisees own the stores and have a strong say in store management, when a conflict arises with the brand, the brand owner may find it difficult to exert control, risking losing out to the franchisee.

In contrast, HLA adopts a "quasi-direct-selling" model in which HLA franchisees play more of the "financial investor" role, with responsibility for paying expenses but without participation in store operations. In this way, HLA can use the financial strength of franchisees to achieve rapid expansion while maintaining control.

Specifically, after signing a franchise agreement with HLA, a franchisee applies for business and tax registration in its own name. The franchisee has full ownership of the store and HLA does not charge a franchise fee. According to the franchise agreement, franchisees are required to rent a store space with an area of 200 to 500 square meters in a prime retail location in the core business district with a ground-floor street-side facade. The location of the store must be confirmed by HLA headquarters and the franchisee is responsible for the decoration of the store. Before 2014, franchisees even had to pay a security deposit of RMB 1 million to HLA as a guarantee for the goods. When the contract expired and after all financial settlement and transaction issues were complete, the deposit would be returned to the franchisee but without interest. In daily operations, franchisees are obliged to pay for wages, rent and utilities. Those with good connections are also responsible for external management relations with local commerce, tax and regulatory authorities. Through this approach to franchising, HLA has reduced expenses on store rentals, decoration, staff salaries and daily outgoings, and can make use of franchisees' contacts in the local area to overcome obstacles during store opening, thereby accelerating the speed of bricks-and-mortar retail expansion.

In return, HLA developed an enticing profit-sharing model. Before adjustments made in 2014, franchisees would receive as much as 35%, so that for each RMB 100 worth of goods sold at a HLA store, the franchisee would receive RMB 35. After the franchisee paid the rent, utilities, staff salaries and taxes, the rest was net profit. Since the franchisee did not need to pay HLA a fee or bear the risk of overstocking, and did not need to participate in daily management, these settlement proportions were highly attractive.

In HLA's start-up phase, marketing teams had to meet many local entrepreneurs in order to recruit franchisees. Now it is a completely different story: there are more than 2,000 franchisees waiting to open stores, and according to the current speed of store openings, the franchisees at the end of the line may have to wait up to four to five years. The management team of HLA has stated that it will do no more public franchisee recruitment, and all franchisees will be either reinvestments by original franchisees or introductions of relatives and friends. With the strong support of its franchisees, even during the clothing market downturn beginning in the second half of 2015, HLA was able to keep accelerating the speed of store openings, getting their hands on prime retail locations across the country. Zhou Lichen, vice chairman of HLA, said: "We should embrace the opportunity to occupy these store locations now, because they will be very difficult to obtain once the market recovers."

In addition to franchise stores, HLA has also recently accelerated its deployment in shopping malls, because as the business environment changes, consumers are shifting there from elsewhere. In April 2015, HLA signed a "Strategic Cooperation Framework Agreement" with Wanda[7], agreeing that over five years, HLA would play a role in attracting shoppers to Wanda Plazas and, with all other factors being equal, Wanda would give priority to HLA in renting prime locations.

While using franchisee resources to achieve speedy store openings, HLA firmly controls the operating rights through the "quasi-direct-selling"

---

7   A leading commercial real estate operator in China.

model. Taking pricing power as an example: all clothes sold at HLA stores are subject to unified national pricing and are never discounted. HLA headquarters determines the tag price according to a fixed multiple of the purchase price. For example, if the production cost is RMB 100, under the credit purchase model, HLA's purchase price is about RMB 160, and the tag price is RMB 160 times 2.5, which equals RMB 400. In addition, issues such as which SKUs (Stock Keeping Units)[8] should be allocated to the stores, and when and in what quantities they should be distributed, are also decided by the product deployment center at HLA's headquarters after analyzing store daily sales and inventory data. While proposals can be made to headquarters by franchisees, decision-making rests heavily on HLA's central "big data" system. There are usually several major factors considered by headquarters in deciding on volume distribution, including sales in the previous season, plans for new store openings, and growth forecasts for existing stores. If a product sells well, supplementary orders can be issued. In general, once a product has been on the shelves for two weeks, headquarters can roughly predict sales for the whole season and decide whether or not to make supplementary orders.

Leveraging suppliers to improve operational efficiency

Domestic clothing brands in China usually have a very simple "commissioned processing" relationship with suppliers, in which the latter earn a 5% to 8% processing fee. But the gross profit margin provided by HLA to its suppliers is as high as 30-40%. This is because HLA suppliers are actually performing a variety of roles in addition to production, including design, and they bear the risk of returned and unsellable products.

It is hard to believe given HLA's endless stream of new products each year that there are only around 200 designers at headquarters, known to insiders as the "Army Base." The Design Center at HLA's headquarters controls the core elements such as category planning and product development proposals, and outsources non-core elements to suppliers through "joint development," a process which activates thousands of designers employed by HLA's suppliers. The process is as follows: HLA's Design Center serves as

---

8   In the field of inventory management, a Stock Keeping Unit (SKU) is a distinct type of item for sale, such as a product or service, and all attributes associated with the item type that distinguish it from other item types.

the "judge" of product design, putting forward development proposals for all categories of garments and communicating with the design departments of suppliers on concepts and styles. Once product plans are finalized, the suppliers' design teams begin work on prototypes, and the "judge" – HLA's Design Center – makes a preliminary selection, scoring each design from the perspective of the consumer. Only after successive screenings do qualified designs enter production (see Figure. 2). Usually HLA will select 100 designs from thousands of samples and assign orders from the suppliers who provide them.

During the production process, HLA also exercises strict control over suppliers. When selecting suppliers, HLA adopts the "factory audit" model of foreign trading companies, scoring each supplier according to indicators such as financial strength, production capacity, product quality and the dynamic sales rate of each product[9], dividing suppliers into three levels: red, green and black. Red-listed suppliers are granted extra support, more orders, higher purchase prices and higher gross profit margins, allowing them to

Figure 2: HLA's Product Design Process

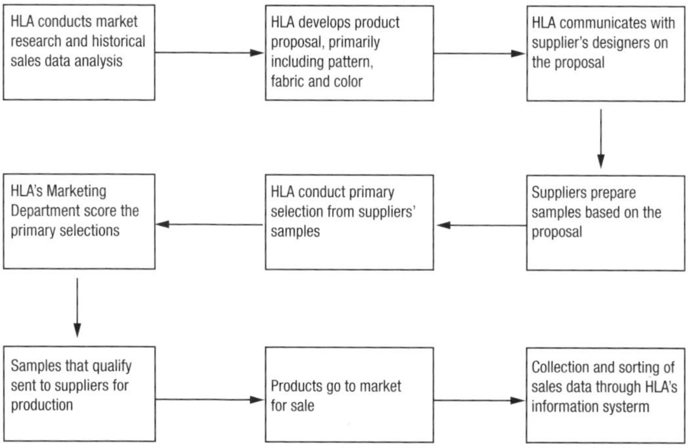

Source: CKGSB Case Center

9 The dynamic sales rate = total sales / total inventory, generally calculated monthly. To check inventory backlog, if the inventory of a certain item at the beginning of the month is 20, with 80 received during the month, and sales of 80, then the dynamic sales rate is 80%. The higher the dynamic sales rate, the better the sales of the product.

expand faster. For green-listed suppliers, existing order levels are maintained, while for those on the black list, orders may be reduced or canceled, or in the worst case cooperation is phased out altogether. HLA also arranges for staff in supplier factories throughout the year to keep track of the production process, workmanship and quality. In addition, suppliers must obtain an independent third-party quality inspection report for their product before it can enter the HLA warehouse, and HLA also conducts a 10% sampling inspection of products. After passing these various "checkpoints," products are warehoused. Because order volume tends to be large, and fashion requirements for menswear are not as high as for womenswear, HLA usually takes about half a year from when an order is made with a supplier to its entry into the warehouse. In the after-sales process, if the customer complaint rate for a certain product reaches 3%, all products from that supplier are removed from the shelf and returned.

In HLA's deal for suppliers, vendors alone bear the risk of returns. Apart from 20-30% of "exclusive sales," all HLA products are sold on a consignment basis. The procurement contract HLA agrees with its suppliers states that HLA may return "unmarketable goods" – usually meaning those unsold after two seasons. Some may be repurchased by HLA and sold on HLA's "Hieiika"[10] platform with their labels cut off for up to 70% discount. The rest are left for suppliers to sort out.

Given the gross profit margin and the risk of returns, for a supplier to break even, a product's dynamic sales ratio has to reach 60% over two seasons. If it remains stable at 70% to 80%, the supplier can sleep easy at night. The higher the rate, the more orders HLA will make with them. The two indicators suppliers care most about are gross profit margin and the dynamic sales ratio. Over the years, the average dynamic sales rate of HLA products after two seasons is more than 70%.

Besides these incentives and elimination mechanisms, HLA has played a leading role in the supply chain since 2012, pushing through major procurement reforms. Specifically, HLA works jointly with its major suppliers to negotiate pricing with raw material suppliers upstream. After receiving discounts, HLA's major suppliers will sign purchasing contracts with upstream suppliers themselves, greatly reducing their production costs.

---

10   A discounted warehouse garment platform.

HLA's core competitiveness

While figuring out how to leverage franchisees and suppliers, HLA is also committed to improving brand marketing, store management, warehouse management and logistics, personnel training and e-commerce capabilities.

In contrast to the regionalized management model adopted by other garment companies, HLA has built a central logistics park and insists on centralized warehousing, centralized management, unified deployment and responsive logistics management, striving to achieve the most efficient logistics network possible. The HLA Central Logistics Park has involved a total investment of RMB 1.6 billion, RMB 500 million of which has been spent on a smart warehouse that opened in 2011. The entire warehousing base occupies an area of 41 hectares, with a construction area of 800,000 square meters and a storage capacity for over 100 million SKUs (Stock Keeping Units), capable of meeting the storage needs of 5,000 stores. HLA has the largest warehousing area and biggest storage capacity in the whole of China's clothing industry. The most eye-catching constructions in the logistics park are 20 highly intelligent logistics warehouses, which deliver nearly a million garments to more than 4,000 stores nationwide every day.

To maximize efficiency, HLA has built a smart high-rack warehouse that can store approximately 1.4 million boxes and 56 million SKUs (Stock Keeping Units), seven times that of a flat warehouse the same size, with all placement and removal handled by stacking machines. The company has linked its sales management system with the logistics information system in real time, and when a certain store reaches the minimum inventory for an item, the system can get a robot arm to pick out the item and send it to the delivery zone within 30 seconds. HLA headquarters delivers to stores twice a week, adjusted based on demand. All stores have a small storeroom for holding inventory, and can transfer goods from surrounding stores if needed. This perfected logistics system gives HLA an accurate and efficient control over the entire supply chain, safeguarding market expansion. As HLA is responsible for warehousing, while suppliers and stores are responsible for transportation, costs to the company are well controlled.

In using the "quasi-direct-selling" model that separates ownership and management rights, the headquarters of HLA undertakes a large proportion of daily store management tasks. HLA has a highly centralized store management approach, which concentrates decision-making power and management rights for the stores with headquarters, implementing unified management in terms of brand image, pricing, procurement, distribution, decoration, recruitment, personnel training and settlement. Managers directly manage stores as frontline executors of the "HLA Standard." HLA has creatively established a "professional store manager" system under which, every time a new store is opened, HLA sends a professional store manager to supervise for the first few months until a competent store manager, supervisor and salesperson have been trained up. An in-store manual for staff ensures detailed standardization of work processes on a daily basis. In order to further ensure the implementation of the standards, HLA has also created a "mystery customer" system, conducting unannounced visits to stores across the country.

From the brand's early days, HLA has left a deep impression on consumers by recruiting celebrity spokespeople, and using all-round advertising and store promotion. With the increase in interactive television programs, HLA has repeatedly participated in the sponsorship of such programs, using its image as China's National Menswear Brand and providing clothing sponsorship to popular entertainment shows such as Zhejiang TV's "Running Man," Jiangsu TV's "Super Brain" and CCTV's "The Great Challenge." Helped by rising ratings for these shows, the brand image of HLA has spread rapidly. HLA has had great success bringing out limited edition versions of clothes worn by celebrities on these shows. While a brand development budget of RMB 500 million per year may not be high, HLA has successfully gained the return it wanted, which is to be one of the big winners behind the scenes.

The company has had high hopes to transform HLA into a management platform for a wide range of fashion brands. In order to achieve this strategic goal, the company's vice chairman Zhou Lichen set out a two-fold direction. First, HLA should upgrade its brand offerings, develop new womenswear and childrenswear, and improve the design and quality of its existing brands. Second, given the current trend of market saturation in China, HLA should make effective use of overseas markets through M&As or market development.

Management believes the biggest challenge HLA faces internally in making headway with these directions is a "talent bottleneck." From fabrics to clothing to brands to future brand upgrades, each transformation places a higher requirement on talent. The development of the company itself is no less the result of talent upgrades. HLA's management realizes that many top talents in the domestic clothing industry live in first-tier cities such as Shanghai, and that it may be hard to attract people to Jiangyin. As a result, the company plans to build a new design center in Shanghai and incubate new brands in regions such as Guangdong, where womenswear and childrenswear brands are concentrated. At the same time, HLA plans to see how it can collaborate more with internationally-renowned IP[11] and designers, and continue to explore new styles. As for overseas markets, they have always been dominated by European and American clothing brands. To access these markets, HLA needs to find suitable overseas acquisition targets and has chosen to employ the strategy of "countryside encircling the cities," starting with markets that are similar to China. The new Malaysian store that Zhou Jianping was rushing to open in late May 2017 was a bold attempt to test the waters. The success of such efforts will also depend on the company's ability to find competent local partners.

Over the past decade or so, HLA's business model has worked well in China, and in the future, HLA will start facing new and mighty competitors such as Uniqlo, ZARA, and H&M in global markets. This will be a huge challenge for HLA's win-win "ecosystem" theory, and will result in an inevitable move to break through development bottlenecks. In a larger sense, this is also HLA's decisive battle to become one of China's most established brands.

---

11 IP is an abbreviation of "Intellectual Property," which refers to intellectual creations – inventions, literary and artistic works, as well as logos, names, images and designs-used in business. Some well-known intellectual property rights represent huge commercial value. For example, if a film company wants to make a Transformers movie, it will need to pay a license fee to the company that owns the Transformers IP.

4. Tujia.com

Bringing Vacation Rentals to China

Supervising Professor: Wang Yanbo; Researchers: Liu Xiaoting, Yang Yan

Despite differences in credit systems and spending habits between China and the U.S., when HomeAway and Airbnb were introduced in China in 2011, domestic entrepreneurs jumped on the vacation rental bandwagon. Airizu Rent was established in June 2011, closely followed by Tujia, Xiaozhu, and Mayi. Just two years later, Airizu had closed. People blamed its failure on it being a blind copy of the foreign model and ignoring local conditions.

Tujia suffered from far fewer growing pains than the other Chinese vacation rental businesses that popped up in this period. The company had a clear target group: middle to high-end Chinese travelers. Six years after its launch in December 2011, Tujia covers 345 cities in mainland China and 1,037 destinations elsewhere, with the total number of listings exceeding 600,000. The company has signed agreements with 217 domestic government agencies and established strategic cooperation with a large number of domestic real estate development companies. Tujia has also signed management contracts for assets of more than RMB 150 billion, providing a potential reserve of 800,000 listings. In 2016, Tujia bought Mayi, and the apartment and homestay businesses of China's biggest online booking platforms, Ctrip and Qunar. At its peak in 2016, Tujia's daily order exceeded 56,000 bookings, a single-day record in China's accommodation-sharing market.

How did Tujia find a way to transplant and adapt the vacation rental business concept to China in just six years?

The establishment of Tujia

The founder of Tujia, Luo Jun, started life as an accountant, later switching to software engineering. He held senior management positions in Oracle, Cisco, and Avaya, and at the end of 2007, founded Sina House[1], completing his transition from professional manager to entrepreneur. In October 2009, Sina House teamed up with E-House China[2] to establish China Real Estate Information Group and to list on Nasdaq.

In 2011, Luo Jun observed that while China's economic growth rate was stable, housing inventory was accumulating and a large number of apartments lay vacant. He also noted that, given "overheated investment" in real estate all over the country, there was the prospect of even more vacant space becoming available. He also noted that with China's rising average incomes, consumer habits were shifting towards cultural and entertainment spheres, especially tourism. A number of large companies in the vertically-segmented system had emerged, meaning that strong demand existed for very specific offerings.

"On one side, I saw a vast supply of vacant housing, while on the other, I saw vast consumer demand for cultural or virtual things," said Luo Jun.

In 2011, the public listing of HomeAway in the U.S. sparked an upsurge in the vacation rental industry. In addition, the shared accommodation model created by Airbnb in 2008 was being readily accepted around the world. Luo Jun saw HomeAway and Airbnb as being basically a match-up of these elements, and since vacation rental was a model that had been proven elsewhere, why not try it in China? While sensing opportunities in the China market, just to be sure, Luo Jun did a round of market research before entering the vacation rental industry.

The vacation rental market

The vacation rental model first started in Europe, where the industry has a history of nearly 100 years, and it also developed early in the U.S., from around 70 years ago. Many Europeans and Americans buy second homes, spend a few weeks there each year and then rent them out for income for the rest of the year. The sales revenue of the industry in Europe and the U.S.

---

1   An online vertical real estate media and information service platform.
2   An innovative and data-based real estate transaction service provider in China.

totaled US$85 billion in 2011, accounting for 37% of total accommodation industry revenues. In Luo Jun's view, China's vacation rental market had only just started and there was huge market potential.

China today has the largest stock of real estate in the world. According to the China Household Finance Survey (CHFS), the vacancy rate of privately-owned housing units in urban areas in mainland China was 20.6% in 2011, much higher than other countries and regions. In the same year, the vacancy rate in the U.S. was 2.7%, and in the U.K. 2.6%.

China was on the way to becoming one of the top markets for global tourism. According to the *People's Daily*, in 2010, the number of domestic tourists in China reached 2.1 billion, an increase of 10.6% year-on-year, and total tourism revenues were RMB 1.57 trillion, an increase of 21.7%.

To succeed, Luo Jun realized he would have to overcome typical Chinese housing market issues. Although housing stock was at an all-time high, little of it was of good quality, in terms of having good facilities and being in a good location, with good transportation links. China's real estate prices had risen so quickly over the previous decade, that property values were high and an unreasonable price-to-rent ratio prevailed. Wealthy Chinese property owners had little incentive to rent out their units. On top of this, short-term rental market operators paid little attention to giving good service and establishing market credibility. Trust in them was very low, so the industry was trapped in a vicious cycle of declining quality.

In the U.S., the boom in vacation rentals resulted from there being a large pool of middle income people who were attracted to participatory tourism. Vacation rentals could provide the experience they craved. In China however, people were still more keen on experiencing the service side of travel, preferring to stay in hotels.

Luo Jun found that in China's hotel market, there were many three-star and five-star hotels but few four-star hotels. Three-star hotels with their low price points were having trouble meeting travelers' rising expectations, while five-star hotel prices were still seen as too expensive. Taking these various factors into account, Luo Jun from the start positioned Tujia at the mid- to high-end of the market, filling the gap created by the relative lack of four-star hotels. Tujia's market segments would be "urban," "tourism," and "special features."

Tujia's opening moves

What was the key to success for HomeAway and Airbnb? Luo Jun discovered that they are rooted in the unique community fabric of the U.S. The U.S. vacation rental industry, after more than 70 years of development, was a completely offline system. Each community has a property management company providing real estate maintenance as well as mature real estate agencies, making it easy for homeowners and tenants to build mutual trust. In addition, there is a relatively complete third-party service system and a well-developed credit rating system. HomeAway and Airbnb simply built an online information exchange and trading platform on the foundation of the existing offline systems using an "asset-light" model.

But in China, merely constructing such an information platform was not enough. There was no mature system that could be relied upon by either the owner of the rental property or the tenant, so it was difficult for the two sides to establish trust. With offline systems still struggling, Luo Jun decided to build Tujia using an "asset-heavy" approach, and do both online and offline business.

Tujia's three-step business model

First step: Gain control of housing resources

The fact that domestic tourists were not yet familiar with the vacation rental idea was in his view irrelevant. Tujia should take firm control of the housing resources before new cultural concepts and spending habits were established, while simultaneously cultivating the growth of the market by offering various types of featured accommodation. In terms of housing resources, Tujia's approach was to cooperate with individual homeowners. Its key innovation was to adopt the model of "homeowner's requirements first," that is, to give priority to protecting the owner's rights to self-use and allowing the homeowner to take back the unit at any time. Tujia only helps the owner to make money when they are not staying in their house.

However, identifying housing resources in such a way is both time-consuming and costly, so based on his many years of experience in the real estate industry, Luo Jun came up with another idea: cooperation with real estate developers. Many second- and third-tier cities in China currently face the problem of surplus housing and developers are very willing to get rid of inventory. For Tujia, this approach not only ensures that the accommodation units Tujia gets are not only situated close together and easy to manage, but are also new and of high quality. Tujia signs an exclusive agreement with a developer under which the developer purchases housekeeper services from Tujia. One year later, when the developer hands over the units, Tujia enters the community and interacts with homeowners in the same manner as a property management company, giving homeowners a commitment on housekeeper services. Owners can also choose Tujia's open trusteeship services under which Tujia will manage the units according to the specific requirements of the homeowners.

For developers, linking a housing unit to Tujia's housekeeper services means not only that the selling price is raised, but it is also easier to sell. As of the beginning of 2016, Tujia had reached cooperation agreements with most domestic real estate developers including Vanke, Wanda, and Greentown, and had signed up 800 projects covering an inventory of 800,000 units, while a further 12,000 projects are under discussion. At present, this method has become Tujia's main channel for accessing housing resources.

In addition, for featured tourist areas such as Lijiang and Dali[3], Tujia also cooperates with mature and distinctive guesthouses, featuring their units on Tujia's online platform in return for a commission. In Luo Jun's view, this approach not only "brings in more platform traffic and orders," but also meets the needs of a certain type of tourist.

After some experimentation, Tujia settled on a two-dimensional screening system for identifying housing resources. One dimension was location, for which there were three criteria: 1. places with convenient transportation such as close to airports, high-speed rail stations and freeway exits; 2. places with nearby tourist attractions, taking into account other factors such as the tourist numbers and distance from scenic areas; 3. saturation of the local accommodation market. Luo Jun believes that since Chinese travelers are used to staying in hotels, other factors such as competition from hotels should be taken into account. Tujia generally does not expand its business in locations with many hotels.

The other dimension is partners, using one of three types of cooperation:

---

3   Both are tourist cities in northwestern Yunnan, China.

1. Cooperation with real estate developers. There are two specific modes: in one, Tujia is involved in the design phase and provides the owner with a rental guarantee, while the other is management of leftover units. For instance, if a developer has constructed four blocks and only sold three, they will not be willing to sell the remaining block cheaply. Given that most of the costs have been recovered, the developer will not be in a hurry to sell and can instead turn the block over to Tujia to operate.

2. Community cooperation. Tujia's accommodation units tend to be situated relatively close together, with at least 50 units in each community (the maximum number acceptable to Tujia is based on factors such as transport facilities, visitor numbers and business frequency). Tujia will choose small-scale business cooperation in locations with which it is familiar, except in locations which already have high occupancy rates.

3. Cooperation with existing players in the vacation rental business. For locations where it is difficult to obtain housing resources, such as in Beijing, because other players are already active there, Tujia will generally choose to cooperate with existing players and allow their units to be placed on the Tujia platform with Tujia providing the orders.

Second step: Improve offline services

Luo Jun believes that to ensure good user experiences, Tujia has to take on the responsibility of improving offline services. To this end, Tujia chose to implement offline services and standards closer to those of the hotel industry, such as using the U.S. Sweetome hotel management system, providing airport pickup, drop-off and pet check-in, offering uniform bedsheets and quilt covers, and cleaning guest rooms.

Currently, Tujia categorizes the services it offers into two types: housekeeper services for properties and open trusteeship services. With both, Tujia has dedicated personnel to handle maintenance and cleaning during periods when the unit is not occupied by the owner. But the the owner can still keep track of maintenance of the unit and any changes to the surroundings through a computer or mobile phone.

The difference between the two is that the time available for Tujia to sublet the unit is limited to the period the owner proposes for exchanging homes. For example, only when the homeowner applies to swap two days' usage of his house in return for one day in another place, is Tujia able to make use of the house without involving a financial transaction. With the open trusteeship service, except for periods reserved by the owner ahead of time for self-occupation, Tujia can access the house at any time and share the rental income with the owner on an agreed basis. In addition, homeowners who select the open trusteeship service retain the right to do exchanges with houses in other locations.

Tujia's housekeeper services are not cheap, with a minimum fee of RMB 6 per square meter per month, which is higher than general property management fees. In general, real estate developers will purchase a three-year housekeeper service from Tujia and pass it on for free to homebuyers when they purchase the unit. Every three years thereafter, the owner and Tujia sign a contract directly. Meanwhile, open trusteeship services involve one-on-one deals, signed once a year, depending on the owner's specific requirements. Under the open trusteeship service agreement, Tujia will put the units on its online platform for rental during the owner's absence, which makes it necessary to conduct a round of renovation to standardize the units at an early stage.

In addition, offline services require an adequate number of staff. In order to control costs, Tujia has adopted a human resource sharing model, redeploying staff across the country to meet peak and off-peak tourist demand. For example, the Spring Festival is the peak season in Sanya[4] but the off-season in Qingdao[5]. In this case, some service personnel in Qingdao are deployed to provide support in Sanya.

Tujia launched a Run By Agent (RBA) service to help homeowners add value to their vacant accommodation, providing assistance from rental pricing to linen laundering. Tujia also launched an "easy stay" service for homeowners, including bedding and toiletry changes after each check-out, plus room cleaning and use of smart door locks to provide consumers with basic conditions of hygiene and safety, and solving homeowner problems such as the training and management of cleaning staff, and providing assistance with their rental operations. Only by resolving such management issues for homeowners can tenants be assured of a better accommodation experience.

---

4   The southernmost city on Hainan Island widely known as "China's Florida", drawing a large number of retirees from Northeast China during winter.
5   A major city in the east of Shandong Province on China's Yellow Sea coast.

Third step: Attract users

In the early stages, Tujia adopted cooperation with Ctrip. As a leader in the domestic OTA market, Ctrip not only offered Tujia access to a resource of tens of millions of members, but also launched a dedicated channel to facilitate the diversion of traffic flow towards Tujia. Later, Tujia continued to strengthen this advantage and today its orders exceed the resources provided by Ctrip.

Tujia's user groups fall into three categories. The first is business travelers who mainly choose accommodation near the CBD (Central Business District) area; the second category is tourists, including visitors to nearby attractions and destinations; the third category is people who choose villas and featured accommodation. Tujia's data analysis shows that 70% of people staying in Tujia accommodation are on family trips, 10% are on couple vacations, 10% are friends' gatherings and 10% are business travelers.

Strategic partnerships

Luo Jun has been on the lookout for partners since the start. The first goal was to cooperate with real estate developers. In April 2012, Tujia signed its first strategic agreement with Shimao Property, opening the door to different cooperation models with real estate developers, and in November 2015, Tujia signed an agreement with Shoukai Group, a leading Beijing real estate player. With Shoukai Group, Tujia established "Housekeeper Trusteeship" services, project marketing and other innovative businesses.

As of March 2016, Tujia had concluded cooperation agreements with 80% of the top 100 real estate companies in China. Luo Jun believes that the benefits of such cooperation are obvious. Obtaining control of housing resources directly from the primary market is both simple and convenient, and ensures centralized supply and a high quality of accommodation. From the perspective of the developers, faced with overcapacity as the real estate industry moves beyond its "golden era," the Tujia model can help boost sales and improve after-sales service, thus reducing the pressure of vacant inventory. In addition, Tujia can also help owners maintain and add value to their properties, while providing travelers with cost-effective accommodation.

In line with the same win-win principle, Tujia also collaborates with local governments. For example, in December 2015, as part of its cooperation with the government of Jiangshan in Zhejiang Province, Tujia proposed that in addition to expanding the number of holiday apartments in the Jiangshan area, it would offer preferential prices on travel products, including scenic spot tickets, dining and transportation through the Tujia online platform. For local governments, Tujia's innovative model not only helps to increase fiscal revenue and solve the problem of local employment, but also can stimulate local property sales and boost the local tourism market. Encouraged by these benefits, many local governments have taken the initiative to seek cooperation with Tujia. Since the signing of the first strategic cooperation agreement with the Shandong Tourism Bureau in October 2013, as of September 2017, Tujia has entered into cooperative relationships with 217 local governments.

In addition, HomeAway, one of the world's largest vacation rental providers and one of Tujia's shareholders, places selected overseas listings on Tujia.[6] Ascott, a top international serviced residence owner and operator which participated in Tujia's fourth round of financing, also formed a joint venture with Tujia and in 2016 launched a joint brand called Tujia Somerset. In 2016, to further expand the business, Tujia also acquired Mayi short-term rental, as well as the homestay business of Ctrip and Qunar.

On October 20, 2016, Tujia announced a strategic agreement to acquire the apartment and house rental operations of Ctrip and Qunar, transforming Tujia from a single platform into a matrix of four platforms: "Tujia, Mayi, Ctrip, and Qunar." With one leap, it became a giant in the accommodation sharing industry. Through its Tujing app, Tujia has gradually opened up the housing inventory of each platform to allow for the sharing of housing resources. Homeowners can manage their rental units on different platforms through a unified back-end system. This not only improves operational efficiency, but also guarantees huge traffic flows.

Tujia's mixed model

It should be pointed out that the introduction above mainly refers to Tujia's self-operated B2C model. In fact, through the process of localization, Tujia has formed a mixture of three models by "borrowing" some elements from

---

6   HomeAway's vacation rentals selected for inclusion on Tujia.com are in the most desirable destinations for Chinese nationals traveling abroad, including homes in Australia, Western Europe, Southeast Asia, and the U.S.

Table 1: Comparison of the Three Business Models

	Self-operated B2C Model	Small B2C Model	C2C Model
Main Features	Tujia controls housing resources and provides offline services in line with industry standards for star hotels	Tujia only serves as the platform	Tujia only serves as the platform
Housing Resources	Collaboration with developers	Third-party hotel operators	Private owners
Start Time	December 2011	December 2011	Early 2015
Profit Model	Revenues shared with homeowners	Commission fees	Commission fees

Source: CKGSB Case Center

both HomeAway and Airbnb (see Table 1).

The first is the self-operated B2C model. As mentioned above, the characteristics of this model are that listings are controlled by Tujia in cooperation with developers, while offline services follow Sweetome standards. Luo Jun hopes that high-quality listings and services will help Tujia establish its brand image. At present, the revenue generated under this model is shared 50-50 between Tujia and the owner, with a small portion divided either 60-40 or 70-30.

The second is the small B2C model. In this model, the accommodation units are provided mainly by third-party merchants, Tujia only serves as an open platform, with offline maintenance and pricing being handled by the operators themselves. Luo Jun believes that opening up Tujia's platform to third parties helps to expand the volume of housing resources available, especially in areas with low coverage, while products such as Blossom Hill[7] can also add a lot of new features to the platform. At present, revenue under this model comes mainly from a 10% commission per order.

The third is the C2C model. In much the same way as Airbnb, Tujia serves only as a platform to match transactions between homeowners and tenants, and generally charges a commission. But Tujia also offers many additional services, for example providing guidance to owners with newly-released units

---

7   A Chinese guesthouse brand.

on how to decorate, arrange and photograph their units, helping them to achieve a high occupancy rate and better management of their rental business. Meanwhile, in order to improve the user experience, Tujia has set up an offline team to verify the quality of listings and the authenticity of reviews.

In Luo Jun's opinion, the C2C model has two advantages: First, it can compensate for deficiencies of the self-operated B2C model; second, it can create interactions between tenant and homeowner in the manner of Airbnb. However, there are still many problems with the development of the C2C model in China, such as a lack of a way to guarantee the quality of accommodation and the lack of trust between homeowners and tenants. Luo Jun has consciously controlled the pace of expansion of the C2C business, because he wants to show the potential of the market through Tujia's operations and allow people to gradually accept the model by working to establish rules and regulations for the industry, and optimizing the user experience.

According to iResearch, Tujia has a total of 450,000 online listings, of which approximately 30,000 are self-operated (B2C), about 20,000 are from private home owners under the C2C model and most of the rest – about 400,000 listings – are from third-party merchants (small B2C operators). But since these third-party merchants are not using only the Tujia platform, the transaction volume is not proportional to the number of listings available. Actually, most of Tujia's orders come from business under the self-operated model.

Establishing a system of trust

In working out its business model, one of Tujia's biggest breakthroughs was setting up a system whereby it could gain trust, addressing a key cause of the slow development of China's short-term rental market. Homeowners tend not to trust third parties and are not comfortable handing over their homes for management. Moreover, a lack of integrity can develop into a poor tenant experience. In particular, inconsistencies between accommodation and the pictures displayed result in the tenant losing trust in the rental platform.

In response to these problems, Tujia has used mobile technology to initiate a system of trust based on information symmetry. This is three-fold.

The first part is winning the trust of the homeowner through a confirmation arrangement. Tujia sees the major concern of homeowners being that the third party may rent out the accommodation but not declare it and hide the income. To address this, Tujia launched a website for homeowners showing a detailed schedule for each listing, so they can check at any time if the place is rented out. Homeowners can also log into the visitor website and check that the information is consistent between the two websites. If the homeowner website shows the unit as being rented, but the visitor website shows vacant, then a repeat order placed will cause problems throughout the entire system. Luo Jun points out that this approach is similar to audit checks in accounting.

The second part is winning customer trust by providing services to enhance information symmetry. Tujia has explored several approaches:

1. To ensure that all uploaded photos are real and have not been photoshopped, Tujia has set up an offline team to take pictures rather than let homeowners do it.
2. As each unit is unique, the Tujia website provides a floor plan for each one, showing area, layout and specific indicators such as window size.
3. If the customer feels on arrival that a unit is different from the photographs, and as long as that is in fact the case, Tujia immediately provides compensation.
4. The Tujia call center will call customers within two hours of their departure asking for feedback, and take action according to the feedback.

The third part is achieving information symmetry through a real-time big data sharing platform. Owners want to know if they can take back their house at any time and customers want to see the overall housing information. Luo Jun believes that to achieve these requirements, a real-time big data sharing platform is essential. On the customer side, Tujia has established a website and mobile app, while for the owners, Tujia has also set up a dedicated website. To handle back-end price management as well as guest check-in, check-out and payment, Tujia has also developed its own VRMS – Vacation Rental Management System. There is also a call center system. These systems all share the same big data platform, as a result of which, users can accurately execute searches or reservations in real-time.

A competitive future for Tujia

How to maintain the pace of expansion of the C2C business? How to compete in a differentiated way with Airbnb and HomeAway in overseas markets?

How should Tujia respond when other large Internet companies decide to enter the non-standard accommodation field?

"We do both online and offline, and those who only do online cannot be considered our rivals," Luo Jun said. But in fact, on a larger scale, Tujia faces a wide range of competitors.

Xiaozhu: In terms of C2C business, Xiaozhu is probably one of Tujia's potential competitors. Like Airbnb, Xiaozhu mainly serves as an online platform to facilitate transactions between individual homeowners and tenants, with revenues coming from the collection of a certain commission from homeowners, averaging about 10% of accommodation rates. Its targeted customer groups are mostly people traveling for sightseeing, study, medical treatment, and job hunting, to whom it provides short-term accommodation options that are cost-effective and have a friendly atmosphere. At the end of 2016, Xiaozhu completed its C+ and D rounds of financing, totaling US$65 million. The platform now has over 200,000 listings in 306 cities in China, with over 1,000 published every day.

Airbnb: Airbnb, a founder of the shared economy concept overseas worth upwards of US$31 billion, poses a certain threat to Tujia. Having already entered 191 countries worldwide, Airbnb announced its plans to enter the Chinese market in partnership with Sequoia Capital and China Broadband Capital in 2015. By November 2016, Airbnb China went live. Airbnb has approximately 80,000 accommodation listings in China and has arranged stays for over 1.6 million domestic and foreign travelers. Still relatively small-scale, Airbnb plans to boost its R&D capacity and investments in China so as to effectively localize its business strategy.

BAT and other Internet Giants: China's three Internet giants, Baidu, Alibaba, and Tencent, have aggressively expanded into online travel and accommodation. As early as May 2010, Alibaba launched the Taobao Travel Platform, providing consumers with one-stop independent traveler services. After an upgrade, the service now called Fliggy provides ticket sales, hotel reservations and vacation packages. Tencent launched a travel booking platform, QQ Tour in 2010 and subsequently made several acquisitions. Baidu launched Lvyou.baidu.com in 2011 and made a strategic investment in Qunar. In October 2015, Baidu swapped Qunar shares for a stake in Ctrip, placing both Ctrip and Qunar, the two biggest online travel agencies, in its camp.

In the area of online short-term rentals, the BAT giants currently still primarily provide standard accommodation products and services and do not pose a threat to Tujia. But considering their wealth of traffic resources, plus the ability to integrate a variety of other businesses in their ecosystems to provide a full range of tourism services, they may have an impact on Tujia once they move into the non-standard accommodation field.

In the past six years, Tujia has experienced rapid development, and Luo Jun has his own ideas about the future direction of the company. After completing D and D+ rounds of financing, he decided to launch three major business lines:

1. C2C business. After preliminary tests, Luo Jun scaled up the business, extending the different product lines by expanding both the scale of housing resources available and the range of special features offered.
2. "Tujia tribe" program. Tujia hopes to develop cooperation with upstream and downstream companies and establish an ecosystem in the non-standard accommodation field, investing in rental platforms and working with partners to expand the overall market.[8]
3. Further expansion of its overseas business. Luo Jun says that Tujia will set up direct subsidiaries in foreign destinations to meet an ever-growing vacation demand from Chinese users. Until now, Tujia's overseas listings mainly came from its partnership with HomeAway. In early 2017, Tujia turned to Relkux, Japan's luxury booking site, to enrich and expand its offerings. In August 2017, Tujia and the vacation rental provider of Rakuten Group[9], entered into a partnership, with Tujia permitted to cross-list Rakuten properties in its overseas vacation section.

While the domestic market is very competitive, Tujia has managed to survive by addressing consumer needs and concerns, building up a strong level of brand trust and forming successful partnerships. Internationally, bookings in the first half of 2018 for outbound travel by Chinese users of Tujia grew more than tenfold over the same period the previous year, and Tujia also has the opportunity to take advantage of the continued strong growth in overseas tourist travel by Chinese people.

---

8   In 2015, Tujia invested in 52xiaoluo.com and 51wofang.com. In early 2016, it concluded a strategic cooperation agreement with Weshare. Tujia plans to keep absorbing partners into its ecosystem.
9   Rakuten LIFULL STAY.

5. Haier

Haier's Digital Transformation

Supervising Professor: Li Yang; Case Researcher: Deng Di

One day in 1985, Zhang Ruimin, then director of Haier's predecessor, Qingdao Refrigerator Co., summoned his staff to the factory yard so they could watch as 76 defective refrigerators were smashed with a sledgehammer in front of their eyes. From that day, this Qingdao factory's fortunes would change dramatically. Poor quality and consumer complaints would no longer be tolerated. Zhang Ruimin would change the company's name to Haier, and encase the sledgehammer in glass as a cultural relic. Haier would be revived from a dying collective small factory to one of the largest white goods[1] brands in China and in the world. For eight consecutive years from 2009, Haier held the largest retail market share of any household appliance brand in the world.[2]

As an entrepreneur who personifies China's reform zeitgeist, Zhang Ruimin foresaw how the Internet would make waves, and was adamant that all companies had to "find the fastest way possible to turn into Internet enterprises." In 2012, Haier announced a new online strategy.

From smashing fridges, Zhang now wanted to "smash" the structure, dismissing 10,000 mid-level managers and turning Haier's pyramid organization into a flatter one – Platform hosts were set up to perform the task of building and supporting innovation teams, and small and micro sub-companies were created, peopled by employees in the new guise of eager entrepreneurs. The aim was for Haier to develop an internal corporate

---

1   White goods refers to refrigerators, washing machines, air conditioners etc., products used for housekeeping tasks. Such appliances were originally usually housed in white enamel-coated steel casings, hence the term "white goods."

2   Haier. (n.d.). About Haier. Retrieved from http://www.haier.net/cn/about_haier/haier_global/global/

structure that would simulate the relationship between investors and entrepreneurs, while the company's management team offered business guidance and high-quality IT, finance, and HR services.

To stimulate a culture of entrepreneurship, Haier gave staff more decision-making power. They could recruit and allocate resources according to their departmental needs. Haier employees were encouraged to see themselves as CEOs, at the beck and call of users instead of their corporate superiors. In 2005, to encourage internal startups to interact with users at "zero distance," Haier brought in a new "Users Pay Salaries" remuneration package. It was based on two value dimensions: corporate value, measured by sales revenue, profit, and cash flow, and user value, measured by traffic, loyalty, retention rates and active user numbers.

Figure 1: Company Compensation System Two-Dimensional Model

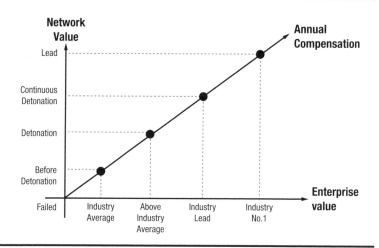

Source: CKGSB Case Center

Haier's new user interaction focus

The new way of managing staff helped Haier come to terms with new trends in the sector. In the face of overcapacity, competition in white goods had shifted from capacity to demand fulfillment. Industry expert Luo Qingqi noted that the household appliance market appeared to be suffering from a lack of interaction with users.[3] User-facing staff were better suited to handle the shift in competition that had taken place in the sector. Haier took up the challenge by seeking to individualize the customer experience. Consumers used to have a completely passive role in manufacturing, involved at the point of purchase and beyond, but isolated from production. Haier wanted to integrate marketing into the production cycle, drawing consumers into the cycle earlier on, so that their needs could be better addressed. Haier called this its "C2M" (customer-to-manufacturer) model – an Internet-driven manufacturing process centered around user interaction. The goal was large-scale, transparent, seamless, visible customization, at zero distance to users.

In 2016, Haier developed a social CRM system[4] and interactive user center. Its back-end platform offers analysis and support, looping back to users and also generating profit goals. Haier identifies its users and what they want by interacting with them and mining their data.

According to the director of Haier's interactive platform, Chen Guoliang, traditional manufacturers sell directly to distributors. There may be no follow-up with users beyond the most basic after-sales interaction. Haier, by contrast, has brought all communication, actions and exchanges into

Figure 2: Haier's Reshaping of the Value Chain to Place Users at the Center

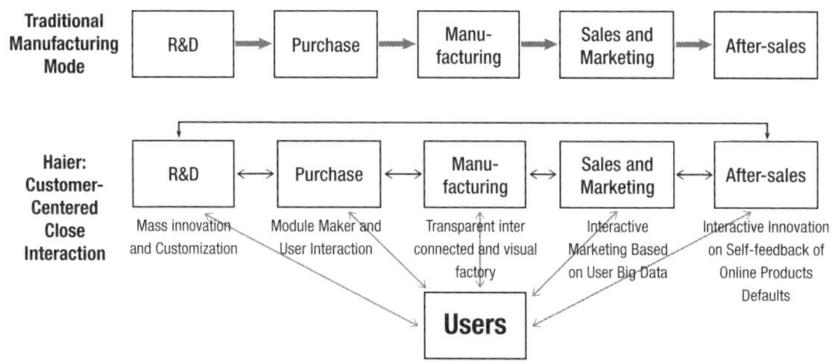

Source: CKGSB Case Center

3   海尔"大事件"交互创新: 从为产品找用户到为用户找产品 [Haier "Big Events" Interactive Innovation: From Finding Users for Products to Finding Products for Users] (2015, December 14), Sina Home.
4   Social CRM, or social relationship management, is customer relationship management and engagement fostered by communication with customers through social networking sites, such as Twitter and Facebook.

consideration by reforming its relationship with users at every stage of the production cycle.

Haier has many touch points with its users, so allocating staff to handle them is hard to juggle. To ensure timely zero-distance interaction, online and offline user touch points are integrated into Haier's interactive user platform. These include social media platforms, Baidu search, Haier websites and forums, the Haier call center, as well as its offline distribution channels. The pool of Haier staff who engage with users now stretches to planning, R&D, marketing, and membership managers. Word-of-mouth promotion and public sentiment monitoring takes place on hundreds of social networks via the interactive user platform. Whenever users post comments on Haier products, they are captured and conveyed to the company's operational divisions or internal startups. Staff can use the platform to interact with users, uploading responses onto social media and the web in real time.

Haier's "Smart Life" strategy

User interaction is essential for Haier's latest expansion into online-operated appliances. Promoted as the "U+Smart Life 2.0" strategy, Haier has made a good start in the promising consumer segment. By the end of September 2016, the company had sold around three million "smart" appliances, accounting for over 10% of total sales. With traditional appliances, user interactions tend to be about hardware quality and value-added services, such as maintenance. But with smart appliances, hardware is just one part. Software and services are just as important, so building a user community and ecosystem is essential.

An example of how this works is the Linkcook refrigerator.[5] Its inbuilt 10-inch LCD screen enables users to watch videos, find recipes manually or by voice search, place produce orders or manage stock. The fridge connects to other Haier products including range hoods and gas stoves, and adjusts fan speed or heat level automatically depending on what is being cooked. Over 30 product and service providers work with Haier to advertise on the screen (at users' discretion). Users can interact with their fridge via the "U+" or Linkcook app, uploading and sharing photos or they can connect with other users on the product's online forum. All this information is fed into

---

5   Xinchu馨厨 refrigerator.

Haier's interactive user platform for background analysis, which can be used to predict or preemptively fix any product failures. In 2016, smart fridge sales were forecasted to reach 40,000 units[6].

In the future, Haier wants every home appliance to act as a data sensor, providing real-time feedback to the cloud that includes environmental data, appliance data and user activity data. Meanwhile, third-party resources are being introduced to provide users with all-round value-added services, creating an intelligent home ecosystem.

"No data, no marketing"

In June 2012, Haier launched a unified membership system, "Mengxiang+"[7], and in 2016 its social CRM system. Identifying and building up user profiles marked the beginning of the development of customized services and precision marketing. The vast amount of data generated has been managed by Sun Kunpeng, director of Haier's user data platform. With all user touch points linked for data interoperability, Sun created unified standards and performed unified user verification. Prior to 2012, user data was stored in isolation, and there was no corporate-level platform or unified membership system. By 2016, the Mengxiang+ system had over 42 million members, making it Haier's main aggregation point and most important source of data. The social CRM system has accumulated data on 140 million users, stored 1.96 billion pieces of cookie information and constructed a seven-tier user tagging system with various categories and data models to support precision marketing and interactive innovation.

Sun Kunpeng explained the thinking behind the Haier data platform. "First, the essence of data is people. Second, the value of data lies in its connectivity. Third, data should be used to drive business operations. Fourth, the vitality of data lies in providing services to users."

Data is cold but the people behind it have feelings

The data platform should be built on insights about, and concern for, the users behind the data. There is a saying among Haier staff: "Receiving payment is

---

6   From Haier's interim 2016 annual report.
7   Mengxiang Jia 梦享+

Figure 3: Planned Unified User Center

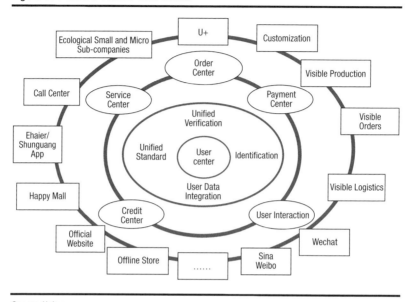

Source: Haier

not the end of the transaction, but the beginning of the interaction." Haier manages its user data on two levels. The first is the underlying data platform covering 140 million Haier users, and the second is Haier's membership system, Mengxiang+, for Haier's core user-group. Mengxiang+ has 42 million members, 8.25 million of whom are active. New members are added at the rate of 30,000 per day, with a monthly retention rate of around 20%. The membership system has alliances with over 30 companies that offer benefits. This is particularly effective for high-end branding. For example, consumers of Casarte, Haier's stylish electrical and kitchenware brand, are members of Mengxiang+. Each Casarte buyer is targeted through multiple precision interactions, and offered incentives to recommend products to others. As a result, Casarte has successfully secured 16 buyers, realizing sales of RMB 180,000. Haier spent only RMB 899 on the initial user, yet received a 200 times return on investment, at least twice that of regular marketing practices.[8]

---

8   According to statistics from Haier, the direct cost of user acquisition for the Mengxiang+ club is zero, and the indirect cost can be RMB 6 per user, cashed out in reward points.

Isolated data has no value

Only by linking isolated data can an enterprise conduct big data analysis and gain useful insights into user behavior and needs. Sun Kunpeng's first step was to integrate the member registration data, user interaction data, sales data and after-sales data that had been dispersed among information systems managed by various departments. There were objections from some departments on the grounds of wanting to retain control, but Sun was able to show them there was no conflict of interest because, thanks to Haier's "Users Pay Salaries" concept described above, each department's interests were determined by the value they delivered to users, not by how many assets they held.

The real challenge has been how to ensure that employees of all departments had the same "digital first" mindset. For instance, operations staff generally found it hard to understand the need for data integration, and Sun and his team did considerable cross-departmental communication work to counter this. They found that the best way was to let outcomes speak for themselves, showing how data generated profit. As a result, interconnected data now links all Haier departments.

360-degree user profiles

The Haier social CRM system identifies each Haier user by name, phone number, address, and purchased product. The data is cleansed and connected up with Acxiom's Audience Operation System (AOS)[9] which, on the precondition that user privacy and information security is protected, acquires user data from social media and retail partners. Users are then tagged to generate a 360-degree user portrait. The social CRM system has collected data for 140 million real-name and 1.9 billion anonymous users. These 360-degree user profiles mark location, demographic, interests, hobbies and preferences for brands and products. The information is categorized using over 600 million data tags.

---

9   Acxiom is a marketing services and technology company focusing on consumer data and database marketing. Its product AOS is a software-as-a-service offering that combines data from multiple sources and enables digital marketers to run analytics and applications against this data to target audiences.

Figure 4: Haier User Personas

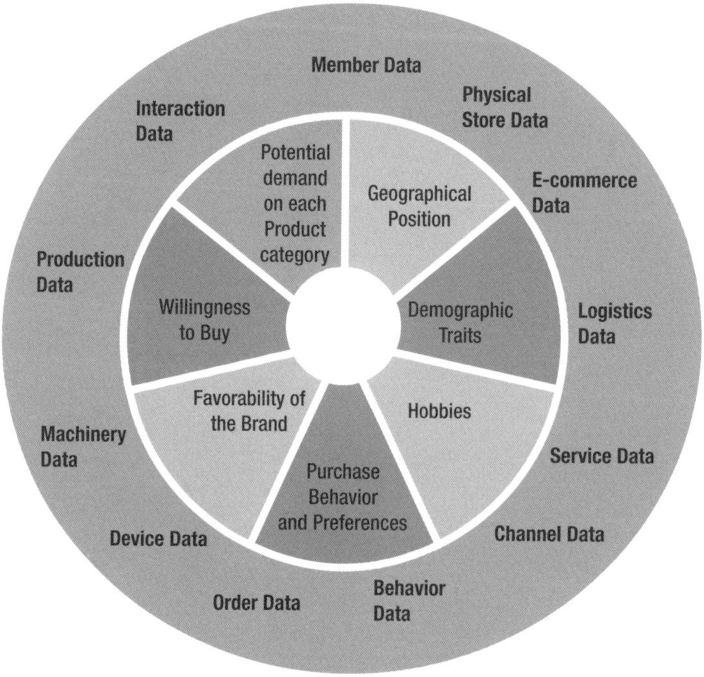

Source: Haier

Proactive fault alerts: Haier gets smarter

With each smart appliance sold, Haier records user and device identifiers and the product code. If anything malfunctions, information is automatically sent to the cloud, so Haier knows precisely what went wrong. Haier proactively contacts users to alert them to any problem, instead of waiting for them to call customer services. Sun Kunpeng says that users tend to be pleasantly surprised at this level of service.

By leveraging comprehensive user details, Haier can provide premium services. The user data platform tags people according to their level of membership and activity and, when a service request is received, Haier's system sifts through its datasets to quickly identify the user, and provide him or her with privileges and personalized attention.[10]

The use of data lies in its ability to serve users

As Sun puts it, "Whatever situation customers are in, we need to offer them the right products or solutions at the right time and place." Ten data models have been built into the social CRM system to predict user demand. Other models, such as the user activity model, assess users according to the frequency, channel and method of their interactions with Haier, and provide higher-level users with increased relationship maintenance.

Haier divides user interaction scenarios into online (browsing, e-shopping, social networking) and offline (home appliance services, store shopping, phone communication), channeling its offers of data services and products through its user data platform. Online, Haier focuses on precision marketing. By connecting with outside DSPs[11], Haier's social CRM system can plan automatic digital ad placements. Targeted users are reached via collaborative targeting (CT) and LiveRamp (LR) anonymous user data matching.[12]

Making heat

One notable joint precision marketing campaign was with Sina Weibo[13] and Gome[14] in August 2015. Based on demand forecasting using its social CRM system, Haier predicted that 32.87 million Haier users might want a product upgrade or cross purchases. Haier and Weibo encrypted their user data, and

---

10 For instance, if Haier's system identifies a phonecall as being made by a gold card member, the call will be given priority during peak periods, and assigned to a more experienced customer service representative exclusively serving gold card members.

11 A DSP (Demand-Side Platform) is a system that allows buyers of digital advertising inventory to manage multiple ad exchange and data exchange accounts through one interface.

12 Collaborative Targeting is part of Acxiom's Audience Operating System that joins client data with ad publisher knowledge to enhance marketing messages. Haier's data partner, Acxiom, acquired the U.S. company LiveRamp in 2014 to help achieve more accurate matching of online and offline user data, more optimized links, and faster identification. The Acxiom Connect product launched on the LiveRamp platform enables anonymous matching and distribution of user data, making multi-channel communication easier.

13 Sina Weibo (NASDAQ: WB) is a Chinese microblogging (Weibo) website. Launched by Sina Corporation on August 14 2009, it is one of the most popular social media platforms in China.

14 One of the largest electrical appliance retailers in mainland China.

performed anonymous matching using Acxiom[15] and found 5.18 million matched users. Haier and Gome then collaborated on a marketing plan and delivered ads to this group of users on Weibo's digital advertising platform, *Fensitong*. Of these 5.18 million matched users, 1.27 million viewed the precision marketing ad on Weibo, and 5,713 bought Haier home appliances through Gome online or offline stores, a conversion rate of 0.45%, which was twice the conversion rate of those in the group of 5.18 million who had not viewed the ad. Sun Kunpeng says that, "This is probably the most complex data-based, cross-brand, cross-platform precision marketing campaign ever carried out by a Chinese company."

Haier's precision marketing is in essence a B2C model with enhanced efficiency. An innovative C2B model is in the works. Haier used to communicate with users through questionnaires to collect data for the R&D process, but the data gathered was often inaccurate or useless. Sun believes Haier's precision marketing predictions for e-commerce channels have been 30% more accurate than traditional marketing methods. He puts this down to Haier's emphasis on serving users, rather than simply achieving sales goals. Haier uses two tools to carry out precision marketing and make full use of active users' enthusiasm, a marketing app and an interaction app.[16]

The marketing app leverages the data analysis and forecasting model of the user data platform to develop precision marketing plans at regional, community and individual levels. It has three major features: the community heat map, the user heat map and the broadcast station. The community heat map is powered by demand prediction models from Haier's user data platform, offering marketers visualized volume and demand forecasts for Haier users in the vicinity, allowing them to recognize high potential communities and plan offline marketing campaigns more effectively. The user heat map, meanwhile, provides information on the volume and real-time demands of Haier users within a radius of five kilometers, allowing marketers to send messages to targeted users to promote Haier products that may meet their needs. User data remains anonymous, with messages sent from the data platform instead of individual phones. The broadcast station helps Haier's sales teams communicate with users in their area using volume and demand data. For an optimal user experience, Haier limits the frequency and content of messages sent out. Diverging from traditionally scattered

---

15   Acxiom, Haier's data partner, acquired the U.S. company LiveRamp in 2014 to obtain the ability to handle anonymous matching and distribution of user data across multiple channels.

16   Yingxiaobao营销宝 and Jiaohubao交互宝.

marketing methods, Haier hopes to create a peer-to-peer marketing model that can deliver useful information to targeted users at the right time, such as when they may need to buy new products and related services.

Haier's interaction app has been designed to help the company better understand users' needs and what they think about its products. The app contains a radar for active users, which utilizes the user activity data model to help Haier's product developers recognize and reach active users. These users are then invited to try new Haier products. Based on big data mining and analysis of after-sales information, the customers' pain point radar pinpoints issues users may have with products they have purchased. The user preference radar analyzes Haier's sales data for health, energy, environmental protection and technology related preferences. Finally, the user life circle function tracks and analyzes topics Haier users discuss on social media, providing a better understanding of who they are, what they like, and who they are influenced by. The rich tapestry of data produced strengthens precision branding and advertising.

The role of third parties

To build the user data platform, Haier has sought support from third-parties. These partners fall into four brackets: First, data strategy and planning partners help Haier clarify application scenarios and the underlying value of the data. Second, partners assist Haier with the collection, cleansing, integration and tagging of data, and provide access to it via an application programming interface. Third, partners in scenario-based algorithm modeling and intelligent data construction build models to visualize information. Fourth, partners in data and application visualization design user-facing apps.

Haier spends four times more on traditional marketing than on precision marketing. Its successes so far suggest reprioritizing to place more emphasis on interaction, content generation and programming. Haier is beginning the process of swapping out traditional hard-sell advertising for soft-sell promotion created with enhanced consumer awareness, in order to improve brand marketing. This will take the form of in-show ad placements, online media and "we-media."[17] Haier's consumer-centric digital transformation is part of an overall ecosystem development.

---

17 "We-media" is known in China as online news sources run by individuals or small groups, often by non-professionals or on a part-time basis.

The most important step towards zero distance

The Internet fundamentally changed the production and management landscape, as traditional labor divisions were broken down. It brought with it information asymmetry and decentralization. Customers now have greater choice and influence regarding the products they buy, and are often intent on seeing their desires satisfied. With the shrinking transactional distance between company and customers, agents have been made redundant as everyone moves closer to the brands themselves. Companies are now far more interested in finding ways to collaborate with each other than in looking inward to strengthen their internal cohesion.

Zhang Ruimin said, "The Internet era is not about what we do or our understanding of customers, but rather about melding the company with the customer. The key concepts are zero distance, decentralization and distributed operations. It is these attributes that help deliver the best user experience possible."[18]

Big data management is the most direct reflection of Haier's "consumer-centric" transformation, but it is just a small part of the company's Internet-driven internal reforms. From R&D to manufacturing to the value chain as a whole, all Haier's processes are being reconfigured around user demand, so that the company can reduce its distance from users and better respond to their needs.

---

18 Haier. (2015). CEO讲话 [CEO Speech]. Retrieved from http://www.haier.net/cn/about_haier/ceo/ceo_speech/201502/t20150207_260454.shtml

6. Ucommune

Breaking Down the Office Walls in China

Supervising Professor: Teng Bingsheng; Case Researchers: Mei Xinlei, Yang Yan

I n the last decade, the rapid development of mobile Internet in the context of globalization has given rise to a new economic model, the sharing economy. How has this model made itself a home in China? Under what conditions has it flourished? Real estate entrepreneur Mao Daqing had a strong hunch that the sharing economy would reshape his industry, boosting both supply and demand, and he decided to ride the wave rather than be swallowed by it. This is his startup story.

Where did Mao Daqing get his inspiration?

A senior manager at one of China's largest real estate developers, Vanke Group, Mao Daqing watched closely as Airbnb took off in the US, shifting resource allocation considerations for companies and the work-life balance for many people. He watched even more closely as, in the US, a flagship of the sharing economy launched in his sector, property management. He noted that the "co-working office space" leasing model represented by WeWork was being wholeheartedly welcomed by the market, with WeWork alone worth US$ 5 billion in 2014 and US$ 20 billion by mid-2017. WeWork's rapid rise pushed the "co-working space" to the forefront of the sharing economy. The sub-prime mortgage crisis of 2008 and 2009 had seen American commercial buildings rake up vacancies and a fresh batch of freelancers and entrepreneurs spill out in the market. The co-working office space model sucked up the idle social and spatial resources that arose from the wreckage and supported the reshaped work patterns that emerged.

Mao Daqing felt China's commercial real estate market was in a similar bind. Vacancy rates for commercial office buildings were high in China too, and the boom in small and micro businesses (SMBs) were sure to provide ample market demand for co-working spaces. Mao heard the government's cry for "mass entrepreneurship and innovation" and in April 2015, resigned from Vanke to set up UrWork[1], a co-working space and startup incubator provider of office space and associated services to entrepreneurs, startups, micro-sized businesses (SMBs) and freelancers.

Two years later, Ucommune had completed its pre-C round of financing, taking in a total of RMB 1.2 billion in funding. It had signed up 100 locations in 30 cities around the world, bringing together more than 4,000 companies and 50,000 members. Occupancy rates were between 60% and 85%, and more than 200 companies in 21 industries were represented. The top three industries were: Internet and technology (40%); cultural and creative categories (23%); finance and taxation (10%). As for financing, in 2015 alone, it helped its resident companies raise nearly RMB 2 billion. Is it safe to say that the company had proven to be a success? To be convincingly successful however, it needed to develop a strategy and stick with it through thick and thin. Most of all, it needed this strategy to leverage all its resources.

Establishing a strategy for China

The Chinese market was unique in many aspects such as social structure, economic foundations and business environment, and Mao Daqing realized that simply transplanting the WeWork model to China was doomed. Creating co-working spaces in China had to take into account China's particular conditions.

Since state policy encouraging "mass entrepreneurship and innovation" was announced in 2015, "Maker spaces"[2] were seeing explosive growth,

---

1   In 2018, UrWork was required to change its name to Ucommune at the behest of WeWork, a co-working company valued at $20 billion in 2017, after a complaint with New York's Southern District Court, alleging that UrWork is guilty of trademark infringement for operating in the same sector with a "confusingly similar name." This case study will use the company's new name Ucommune throughout.

2   Maker spaces refer to all kinds of entrepreneurial locations including working space, online space, space for interaction and space for the sharing of resources, provided to entrepreneurs using a wide range of social resources. In a broad sense, this includes all kinds of shared office forms, including co-working office space.

and this was fueling co-working office spaces based on the rental of "desks" (workspaces), and startup incubators run by venture investors. In 2015 there were 2,300 shared office space operators in China. However, the industry is still in its infancy. Even in Beijing and Shanghai, vacancy rates were as low as 45%. Chinese domestic operators did not have the income streams that WeWork had, relying on rental fees and government subsidies to keep afloat.

Also, due to differences in culture and working style, the users of co-working spaces in China was quite different from those elsewhere. In his research, Mao Daqing found that more than 50% of co-working space users in the U.S. were freelancers, followed by SMBs and the branch offices of larger enterprises,[3] while in China, the main users were SMBs and startups. The positioning of co-working space operations in China also had to be different from the U.S., with arrangements tailored to SMBs and startups.

"Ucommune intends to put 70% of its energy into co-working spaces, and invest the remaining 30% in accelerator services for startups."

According to Mao Daqing's definition, Ucommune was neither a "leasee" that subdivided office space to sub-tenants, nor an incubator oriented towards business investment. Instead, it met all the "non-5A office requirements"[4] of SMBs and startups, and positioned office space rental as an entry point to the sharing economy.

Developing a new business model

China's market for providing office services to SMBs and startups is a new market opportunity, referred to as a "blue ocean opportunity" in marketing parlance. But as China's entrepreneurial landscape itself is just forming, Ucommune needed to provide services that would address customers' initial business needs, not just for property rental and services, but also for entrepreneurship learning, transaction-matching, legal standardization and financial resource integration, to assist startup residents in areas where they fell short through lack of experience.

Despite being such a new area, China's shared office space market has been large and competitive from the start. To win out, Ucommune needed to develop a nationwide space portfolio quickly. Following an "asset-light"

---

3   2011 Global Coworking Survey.
4   Office automation, building automation, communication automation, fire automation and security automation.

operating framework, Mao Daqing expected to gain a cost advantage through its diversified property acquisition methods and rational space design, and attract customers with flexible lease terms and competitive rental rates.

Ucommune attempted to develop a diversified revenue model that went beyond simple "desk" rental (see Table 1). In this way, it sought to reduce the rental proportion of its revenue. As a platform Ucommune decided not to take a share of service providers' revenues, looking to profit from the value they have brought to the ecosystem instead. Ucommune did this by attracting larger companies and service providers to its co-working spaces to enrich its offering and encourage other companies to move in. Ucommune believed that facilitating meaningful interactions between resident enterprises and service providers would help it develop a rich and attractive ecosystem.

Table 1: Ucommune's Profit Model

Revenue Sources	Specific Profit Models	Current Ratio	Target Ratio
Rent	Rental of offices and desks, both short-term and long-term	About 90%	Below 40%
Basic Office Services	Includes fees for meeting room reservations, IT maintenance services etc.	About 10%	Above 60%
Value-added Services	Various value-added services provided by Ucommune, including fees for training, media (marketing), event sign-ups.		
Traffic Monetization	By cultivating a larger group of members and higher transaction frequency, Ucommune benefits through transaction matching, automatic settlement etc.		
Investment in Company Growth	Investing in companies within Ucommune ecosystem, gaining income from their growth		

Source: CKGSB Case Center

You only need to look at its name to know that Ucommune placed a strong emphasis on the community nature of its business. It wanted to break down restraints created by physical "desk" space, and integrate companies, people and resources in offline areas that could release new demand back into the ecosystem. Ucommune would help companies and individuals find partners efficiently and at a low cost. Information would be gathered on its residents' activities and entered onto the database. This "big data" would in turn enable Ucommune to provide more precise services to its residents and optimize office space utilization.

How Ucommune is funded

Ucommune's strategies cannot succeed without adequate capital support. Since its establishment in April 2015, Ucommune has completed six rounds of financing (see Table 2), to meet capital requirements and seek strategic cooperation.

As with many startup companies, the primary purpose of financing is to address the funding gap between investment and operating cash flow during the company's growth phase. In its early days, with developments in many new locations, Ucommune needed funds for rent, refurbishment and new openings, its online booking system, and its efforts to integrate industry resources. The RMB 200 million raised in the A+ round, for example, was used to fund 15 to 20 new projects in Shanghai, Beijing and elsewhere, launch the Online Transaction Platform and Online Equity Trading Platform, and acquire co-working space operators.

More recent rounds of financing have aimed at expanding strategic cooperation. Companies participating in the most recent Pre-C round included Beijing Capital Land (which hopes to revitalize its holdings though cooperation with Ucommune), Xingpai Group (which is exploring a transition in its business scope towards equity investment and integration of the new economy), AKCOME Group (which will provide Ucommune with access to the health care industry and real estate resources) and Prosperity Holdings (which plans to assist Ucommune in the expansion of its U.S. and other overseas business).

Table 2: Ucommune's Six Rounds of Financing

Rounds	Time	Major Investors	Financing Total	Goals
Angel Round	April 2015	Sequoia Capital, Zhen Fund, Sinovation Ventures, etc.	Tens of Millions RMB	Capital Needs
A Round	September 2015	Hanfor, Gopher Asset, Gaorong Capital	Over RMB 200 Million	Capital Needs
A+ Round	March 2016	Hanfor, Hezhong Capital, Yungpark Capital, Gohigh Fund, etc.	RMB 200 Million	Capital Needs
Pre-B Round	June 2016	Yintai Land, ZRT Capital	RMB 300 Million	Strategic Cooperation
B Round (Twice)	January 2017	Taihe Group, Beijing Baifujia Project Management, Tianhong Asset, Junfa Real Estate, Chuanghehui Capital, Tianming Shuangchuang, Dahong Group	RMB 400 Million	Strategic Cooperation
Pre-C Round	August 2017	Beijing Capital Land, Xingpai Group, AKCOME Group, Prosperity Holdings	RMB 1.2 Billion	Strategic Cooperation

Source: CKGSB Case Center

Strategic investment

In investment terms, Ucommune differs from startup incubators in that it does not primarily aim to become a financial investor in its resident enterprises. In fact, Ucommune's strategic investments are mainly into companies that can enrich the overall ecosystem, and are mostly seed investments in startups. Ucommune tends to play a follow-on investor role, acquiring 10%-20% with the intention of forming relationships with investor institutions and reducing risk through the joint evaluation of projects. Ucommune has so far invested in less than ten projects, and exited none.

Location selection at Ucommune

Given the huge potential but undefined nature of the co-working space model in China, Mao Daqing's first priority was to expand the network and secure more prime locations for its clients. An initial target of 20,000 desks was planned, but ambitions were set much higher. Only on the basis of significant scale did Mao Daqing believe the company would have enough market share and brand impact to establish an ecosystem and community that would allow for the integration of its proffered services. At the heart of Ucommune's network expansion is the quest for high-quality locations.

Ucommune has selected cities with well-developed economic and industrial clusters, active levels of entrepreneurship and large numbers of educated young people. Ucommune began in Beijing, Shanghai, Nanjing and Xi'an, and after more than two years, has expanded to 30 cities at home and abroad including Tianjin, Qingdao, Xiamen, Wuhan, Hangzhou, Chongqing, Kunming, Taiyuan, Chengdu, Hong Kong, Taipei, Singapore, New York, and London. Currently 100 locations are in operation with more than 40,000 desks available. Ucommune plans to set up 160 locations in 32 cities worldwide, providing 100,000 desks, within the next three years.

Ucommune has selected locations so as to make the best use of local resources. Its Beijing spaces include Hailong Mansion·Ucommune in Zhongguancun which leverages the entrepreneurial and innovative atmosphere of the Zhongguancun Innoway[5] project, as well as the resources of nearby universities including Peking University, Tsinghua University and Renmin University. The aim is to build a community based on the Internet, education and the smart hardware industry. The Fangshan University Town project with an undergraduate entrepreneurship theme, is located in a technology park and positioned as Ucommune's flagship space for younger people. Ucommune's space in Sunshine 100 in Beijing's CBD utilizes the resources of major enterprises nearby to build a community focused on culture, media, science and innovation and financial services.

Mao Daqing sees physical space as the vehicle for content and ecosystems. Choosing a large space model is conducive to the scaling-up of resident companies and helps to reduce the loss of customers due to the inability to meet their requirements for extra space as they grow. A large space can also accommodate a richer ecosystem. For example, some Ucommune locations

---

5   Since June 2014, Zhongguancun Innoway has gradually assembled a total of 45 entrepreneur service agencies and totally incubated 1,900 startups.

accommodate companies from more than 20 industries and as many as 40 sub-sectors, providing more opportunities for interactions between companies. Ucommune picks spaces larger than 1000 square meters, averaging 4000 square meters across China. The largest space, Alibaba Cloud + Ucommune, has a total area of 14,000 square meters, occupies four floors and comprises of 1,400 desks.

With the constant expansion of its business scale and improvement of brand awareness, Ucommune has begun to develop diversified models for acquiring locations, working to increase control over operating costs and enhance strategic synergies.

Initially, Ucommune rented directly from owners. Most locations signed in the first half of 2015 were rented at fixed prices, as the company had minimal bargaining power. By the end of 2015, Ucommune could sign up new projects at lower-than-average market prices.

Ucommune began exploring cooperation with Alibaba Cloud and other well-known brands in Beijing, Shenzhen and Tianjin. The model required three partners – Ucommune, Alibaba and the local government. Alibaba gave Ucommune media exposure and resources from its ecosystem, the local government provided subsidies for land, renovations and operating expenses, and Ucommune had overall responsibility for day-to-day project operations and project costs. In this form of cooperation, Ucommune used Alibaba's license to obtain local government subsidies and preferential policies without having to pay Alibaba any license fees.

Ucommune and property owners have also experimented with equity cooperation on individual projects. Under this model, the owner is responsible for providing office space and sharing renovation expenses, in return for which Ucommune transfers a proportion of the project equity to the owner. To safeguard its right to operate a location, Ucommune requires that the equity holding of a property owner does not exceed 49%.

In more recent moves, a strategic investment model in collaboration with major commercial real estate companies has taken shape. In June 2016, Ucommune received a strategic investment from Yintai Land Group, a portion of which was in the form of assets. Yintai invested by providing 10-year leasehold rights on eight locations nationwide plus funds for renovation at a discount. Through its strategic partnership with Yintai, Ucommune has expanded to Chengdu, Wuhan, Ningbo, Hangzhou, Jinan, Hefei and other provincial capitals.

Creating Ucommune's offline communities

There are two major factors at play in Ucommune's pricing system.

1. Costs. Pricing is based on a comprehensive consideration of rent, renovation and operating costs at each location, with differential pricing for open area desks and self-contained offices[6].
2. Benchmarking of prices for comparable spaces, the goal being to find a price range that ensures, from the customer's perspective, that the value of the space and services provided is higher than the price charged.

Ucommune uses celebrity online branding to attract potential customers. For example, for the opening of the Sunshine 100 flagship space, Xu Xiaoping,[7] Yang Lan,[8] Pan Shiyi[9] and other key opinion leaders were invited to participate in a promotional video to enhance brand value. Within 24 hours of the video's launch, online views numbered more than seven million, and over 80% of the location's first phase of 575 desks were pre-booked. Ucommune also attracts customers through existing resident companies. Among them, some are leading players with a strong impact on their upstream and downstream partners. The company Runnar in Ucommune's Sunshine 100 location is a pioneer for "running + tourism" and all of Runnar's T-shirt suppliers have now become Ucommune residents.

Ucommune's multi-level leasing model addresses the needs of different customers while attempting to reduce vacancy rates. Ucommune provides an option for members with long-term fixed needs, and charges a membership fee for fixed periods, the shortest being one month. For non-member users with flexible demands, Ucommune introduced hourly rental on the Ucommune app in September 2016. Ucommune's public meeting rooms and event venues can be booked by both members and non-members. Users can view and choose conference rooms and venues through the Ucommune app

---

6   Generally speaking, the price of an open desk provided by Ucommune is lower than the price of an enclosed-office desk. Taking the Sunshine 100 project as an example, the quoted price of an open desk in the early phase of the project was 2,200 yuan per month, and the office desk price was 2,600 yuan per month.
7   Founder of Zhen Fund and a well-known Chinese angel investor. Prior to Zhen Fund, and in association with Yu Minhong and Wang Qiang, he founded New Oriental Education & Technology Group Inc, the largest education and training organization in China.
8   A Chinese media proprietor, journalist, and talk show hostess. She is the co-founder and chairperson of the Sun Media Group and the Sun Culture Foundation.
9   A Chinese businessman. Presently, he is the Chairman of SOHO China, a Chinese office developer.

by date, project and scale, with a minimum leasing time of one hour.

For Ucommune, space is not only a physical site for operations and a source of cash flow, but also a carrier of "content." Mao Daqing believes that through the design and planning of space, Ucommune can realize the value of space in three ways: meeting the needs of resident companies, providing a comfortable experience for employees, and offering a platform and environment that promotes "communication and sharing."

Overall, Ucommune locations in different parts of China and at different stages of development act as independent and interdependent "communities," making up the key components of Ucommune's ecosystem. With the opening of each specific location, designing the space, improving corporate services and upgrading project management and operational efficiency are all important aspects of strategic implementation.

1. Ucommune addressed how to effectively meet the needs of its clients. At the Sunshine 100 location, Ucommune found that the demand for open desk space was increasing as they expanded, while the occupancy rate of enclosed offices remained low. As a result, Ucommune reduced the proportion of enclosed offices, and worked to better handle space design, for example by using potted plants and cleverly-placed decorations to create a psychological sense of "semi-closed space."

2. Ucommune explored how to provide a comfortable experience for clients. Ucommune's spatial design aims to open up public leisure areas rather than maximize rental income through dense desk configurations. Taking the Sunshine 100 location as an example: its 15,000 square meters of floor area includes a 6,000-square-meter gymnasium, and public leisure areas account for 40% of the remaining 9,000 square meters. At its various locations, public areas include cafes, light dining areas, book bars, supermarkets, theaters, and even medical clinics and baby care rooms.

3. Ucommune considered how to provide an environment that promotes "communication and sharing." In Sunshine 100's Hill Theater, a "seating area" suitable for relaxing, eating and chatting has evolved into a social venue for sharing and discussions between companies. In addition, Ucommune arranges large and small "discussion spaces" everywhere, and turns corners into meeting places with armchairs, lighting, and whiteboards.

Serving the Ucommune community

Ucommune has worked on its own brand personality and competitive edge by providing rich "content" for resident companies. Users of co-working spaces in China are small companies and startups that lack both experience and resources, and Ucommune offers all-round support corresponding to the lifecycles of its resident companies. The services offered by Ucommune can be divided into third-party services and self-initiated services, and further classified as life services, core office services and startup accelerator services (see Figure 1).

Figure 1: Classification of Ucommune's Service System

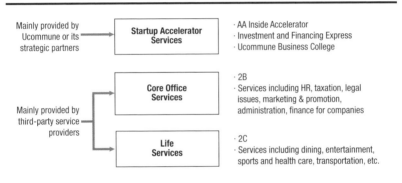

Source: CKGSB Case Center

In addition to its third-party service provider system, Ucommune provided startup accelerator services to resident companies both through internal resources and external strategic cooperation. This includes both entrepreneurial tutoring and investment matchmaking. On August 15, 2016 Ucommune announced its acquisition of a strategic stake in AA Accelerator[10] and the launch of a sub-brand, AA Inside, through which all Ucommune projects can enjoy AA Inside accelerator services. Service offerings include a 12-week accelerator camp to polish its resident companies' strategies and products, and one-on-one targeted counseling and advisory services from the AA Private Board of Directors and resident instructors.

Apart from the service system, Ucommune's main value-added is its

---

10 One of the top incubators in China like Y combinator providing competitive programmes for startups and innovative institutes.

resident company ecosystem. This is the main means by which the company hopes to achieve revenue diversification in the future. Ucommune promotes communication and cooperation among the companies through various in-house activities. Mao Daqing believes the more industries included in the ecosystem, the more conducive it is to communication and business cooperation among companies. He says that "cross-border cooperation is more likely to happen in a pure atmosphere where there is no competition and no conflicts of interest. Under such circumstances, advantageous resources can be shared between enterprises and employees can communicate with each other."

But in fact, interactions among resident companies do not occur naturally, which poses a challenge. Ucommune's operation teams need to be familiar with the business scope and potential needs of each resident company, and seek opportunities to facilitate transactions and cooperation between them. Ucommune also hosts regular in-house activities to create opportunities for communication and sharing between enterprises. Within four months of its opening, the Sunshine 100 project had held more than 260 large and small-scale activities (see Table 3).

Table 3: Partial List of Sunshine 100-Ucommune Themed Activities

Company Development	Ufu job fair, law lecture, investment and financing matching session
Themed events for Startups	Zhen Fund Pitch Day, Roundtable sharing session
Community Sharing	Sharing session for travelers, Sharing session for marathon racer, guitar lessons and music sharing
"Youchenghui"(优橙会)	Sharing of financing and investment experiences, Founders' lunch meetings

Source: BCKGSB Case Center

In the early days, a special department was set up to identify and recruit appropriate third-party service providers, but due to the initial limitations of the offline model and low brand awareness, as well as Ucommune's small scale, it was an uphill battle. By the end of 2015, Ucommune had secured 147 third-party service providers, including 42 national operators and 105 at the regional level, offering 18 different types of service to resident companies (see Figure 2).

Ucommune went about optimizing its approach to recruiting and managing

Figure 2: Ucommune's Third-party Service Providers (2015)

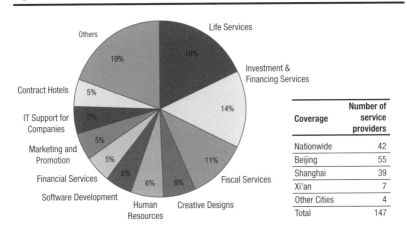

Coverage	Number of service providers
Nationwide	42
Beijing	55
Shanghai	39
Xi'an	7
Other Cities	4
Total	147

Source: CKGSB Case Center, based on information provided by Ucommune

service providers. It established an online platform to process applications from service providers nationwide, and handle transactions between service providers and resident companies regardless of location, thus removing geographical restrictions. At the same time, Ucommune is developing an organic service system that matches services provided by its operations teams, and encourages transactions between resident companies. The scale of third-party service providers has expanded. As of September 2017, Ucommune has signed contracts with 727 service providers.

Building an online community

While expanding and optimizing its offline network of locations, Ucommune has set about perfecting its online systems, and ensuring they are accessible via app or the web. Ucommune wants to make its resources fully accessible online, thereby breaking out of the physical limitation of "desks" to expand the scale of the business and extend the ecosystem. Ucommune's online system primarily covers rentals, services, transactions, networking and big data. Its big data platform is still under development. The online rental system aims to unify and mobilize offline project management and services to improve efficiency and reduce labor and operating costs. It consists of online rental management system, in-house support system and visitor reservation system. The online service and transaction platform includes a service provision platform, investment and financing platform, and an event platform. In addition, an e-commerce platform will launch soon.

The service provider platform allows Ucommune resident companies to contact listed service providers through the app. Resident companies can search for services in twelve categories, including accounting and taxation, financing, legal services, human resources and administration, and then filter service providers according to service coverage area. As startups with limited budget and demand, individual resident companies often lack bargaining power when looking for a service provider, Ucommune therefore hopes to aggregate demand from resident companies.

The investment and financing platform is open to both entrepreneurs and investors, and is not limited to resident companies and large investment institutions. Entrepreneurs looking for financing can post projects on the platform through a simple registration process. Investors can access to all financing projects on Ucommune's online platform after registration and qualification through the Ucommune client interface. Ucommune provides basic services in this process including guidance on the writing of business plans, project reviews, and cooperation facilitation, as well as additional value-added services such as media communications and public relations advice.

The events platform supports event launches, event searches, registration, ticket purchasing, order management and unsubscribing. Most events are open only to member users and are aimed at reducing the promotion costs for organizers while encouraging cross-community activities and motivating resident companies to communicate and cooperate with each other.

The online networking platform is primarily designed not to meet personal high-frequency mobile social interactions[11], but to open up a channel for Ucommune's resident companies to connect with professionals and explore opportunities, thereby enhancing their activity and loyalty. It is only open to members (employees of Ucommune resident companies)[12], and each member is assigned a tag indicating their personal characteristics

---

11 In fact, such high-frequency mobile social demand has been monopolized in China by WeChat and mobile QQ. According to third-party data provider Quest Mobile, by December 2015, WeChat and mobile QQ occupied 33% and 14% respectively of the usage time of all domestic mobile users.

12 This is the situation as of August 2015. Currently, Ucommune has opened the networking platform for all members and non-member users, and non-member users can also post requirements in the Ucommune app.

as well as company information such as location and business scope. The online networking platform allows for searches via tag filtering across the Ucommune ecosystem. Members can also post text or images on the platform to make known their demands or to share information on their own resources and upcoming events. They can have public or private discussions.

Ucommune's online platforms improve the efficiency of offline space utilization and enhance user viscosity and activity. They also allow Ucommune to collect and analyze user behavior, credit and industry data, providing more precise and targeted services for resident companies, member and non-member users, and outside enterprises.

Facing challenges

Starting a business is not easy, as Mao Daqing and his team can attest. After more than two years in business, Ucommune has begun to take shape, but it still faces many challenges. In the short term, Ucommune faces constant cash flow pressure because under its "asset-light" operating model, and unlike operators such as SOHO 3Q, it does not own its property. This means that with both existing projects and new projects, Ucommune faces a stream of cash outflow in the form of rental costs. Ucommune is therefore faced with the need to both cut costs and develop extra sources of revenue.

1. Controlling rental costs is dependent upon whether Ucommune can improve its bargaining power to offset the risk of landlords raising prices, and on whether the company can control the financial burden of opening new projects through diversified location selection models, such as strategic cooperation and strategic investment.
2. With rental income still accounting for 90% of its revenue, a major challenge for Ucommune is maintaining a high occupancy rate. The total average occupancy rate is only 60%, which takes the company close to break-even. Another concern is the state of Ucommune's main customer group, startups, among which the failure rate is as high as 80%.

In the long run, Ucommune's other strategic challenge is how to construct an ecosystem that provides diversified sources of income. According to Mao Daqing's plan, more than 60% of revenue should be generated from service offerings and monetization of the value of the ecosystem, but for now, apart from about 10% of revenue that comes from meeting room reservations and event application fees, the model for revenue diversification is still far from clear.

By connecting offline spaces and online platforms, Mao Daqing hopes to generate a content-rich co-working community for Ucommune in which companies and individuals are bonded through physical and virtual working spaces, benefiting from the sharing of resources and cross-border collaborations based on common culture and values. It is true that the sharing economy, based on value identification, has great commercial potential in the Internet era. For example, based on a sense of shared cultural identity, companies can interact and trade with lower costs, and may even create "chemical reactions" through the sharing of resources and content. But realistically, companies in Ucommune's ecosystem are still at a early stage in terms of the frequency and quality of their communication and cooperation, and interactions rely heavily on intermediary services from Ucommune's operation teams.

Addressing the opportunities and threats presented by the sharing economy and the state policy of "entrepreneurship and innovation," Mao Daqing and his Ucommune are forging ahead with the development of the co-working office space concept in China.

7. Huawei

Ups and Downs in Huawei's Globalization Journey

Supervising Professor: Ou-yang Hui; Case Researcher: Li Mengjun

C onsidering how fast it has grown, it is remarkable that Huawei only ventured beyond the borders of China for the first time in 1996. Its competitive pricing and the ability to respond quickly to customer needs have led the company to create a strong presence in the global marketplace, becoming a world leader in telecommunications.

Huawei began in 1987 as a rural sales agent for Hong Kong-based phone and cable network businesses. The firm took a route to globalization summed up by the old Communist guerilla war strategy of "encircling the cities from the countryside." It had employed this to great success in the Chinese domestic market, starting with easily penetrated rural areas and later moving to the sophisticated urban markets. From Russia to Africa, Southeast Asia to the Middle East and Europe, and all the way to North America, Japan and other regions, Huawei now has a multinational market network and international R&D platform. Huawei has set up business operations in over 170 countries and regions, provides services for 45 of the world's top 50 telecommunications operators and covers a third of the planet's entire population. In 2016, Huawei earned RMB521.6 billion in global sales, of which 55% was generated outside China.

The telecommunications equipment industry in which Huawei operates is highly competitive and long dominated by multinationals such as Ericsson, Nokia, Motorola and Cisco. In 2013, Huawei surpassed Ericsson in sales revenues for the first time and became the world's largest telecom equipment vendor. In both 2014 and 2015, Huawei came top in patents and intellectual property owned by a single company, and in 2016, the Polar Code developed with the participation of Huawei was chosen by 3GPP[1] as the control channel coding scheme for 5G enhanced mobile broadband (eMBB). Today, with its groundbreaking developments in key technologies, Huawei is becoming the leader in the telecom equipment industry. Huawei is widely considered to be the only Chinese private enterprise truly capable of conducting global operations in a mainstream sector, making it a globalization model for other Chinese companies.

But despite its significant success in over 170 countries and regions, Huawei has gone through a series of setbacks in the U.S. market. Since Huawei registered FutureWei Technologies Inc., its North American branch, in Texas in 2001, a number of mergers and acquisitions have been thwarted, and in October 2012, Huawei was forced to withdraw from the U.S. telecom equipment market altogether after investigations by the U.S. Congress. Why is this, and what can be done about it?

Huawei's Globalization Roadmap

Huawei Technologies Co. Ltd. was founded in Shenzhen in 1987 by Ren Zhengfei, who is still its president today. In 1994, the company launched the C&C08, a large SPC[2] exchange that it had independently developed at a price two-thirds lower than its foreign counterparts, and Huawei quickly took over the market. By 1998, Huawei had become China's largest telecom equipment manufacturer.

As a business leader, Ren Zhengfei was curious about the advanced management methods of foreign companies and in 1992, he visited leading multinational firms Alcatel and Siemens. These visits had a huge impact on him. Ren realized that "The road for Chinese companies going out to the world is to fight against the best competitors in the global markets." In 1995, when drafting the "Huawei Basic Law," he explicitly proposed that Huawei should be operated as an international company.

In terms of globalization strategy, Huawei adopted a gradual and indirect approach, first leaving the markets of developed countries alone and using the company's low-cost advantages to expand into developing countries.

1   The 3rd Generation Partnership Project is an organization which aims to fix global specifications for telecommunications systems, including the 3G, 4G and 5G networks for mobile phones.
2   Stored Program Control (SPC) is a telecommunications technology used for telephone exchanges.

By doing so, it could both avoid the various limits to entry in developed countries and also use a low-cost strategy to bypass competition with multinational companies. Only after it had established itself in developing markets did Huawei turn its attention to developed markets.

Early explorations (1996-2000)

In 1996, Huawei received a US$36 million contract from Hong Kong's Hutchison Telecom to provide "commercial network" products with narrow-band exchanges as their core. This was Huawei's first order beyond mainland China, soon followed by orders from Russia and Latin America. In 1997, with the Russian economy in a downturn, the multinational telecom giants withdrew but Huawei took the opportunity to establish a "Beto-Huawei" joint venture with local firms in the city of Ufa, developing a localized model for the Russian market. In 2000, Huawei won two major projects, the Ural Telecommunication Exchange and the Moscow MTS Mobile Network, which marked the beginning of expanded sales in the Russian market.

Huawei began exploring the Latin American market in August 1997 and has since established 13 representative offices in nine Latin American countries including Brazil and Ecuador. Huawei also successfully entered Bangladesh, Pakistan, and India in this period. In the year 2000, Huawei's contracted sales reached US$2.65 billion, of which overseas sales exceeded US$100 million.

Huawei's conclusion from its early experience of overseas market expansion was: 1) Adopt a strategy of "winning through persistence," intentionally avoid developed countries with strong controls, quickly enter developing markets with a low-cost strategy, expand overseas operations and accumulate international experience; 2) Follow China's foreign policy route and focus on non-mainstream markets in Asia, Africa and Latin America; 3) Invite leaders of telecommunications departments in Asian, African and Latin American countries to visit China and Huawei to enhance their understanding of and trust in Huawei.

Breaking into Europe and other developed country markets (after 2001)

After gradually opening up the market in developing countries and accumulating a certain amount of international experience, Huawei turned its attention to Europe. In 2001, Huawei cooperated with well-known local agents and succeeded in getting its 10G SDH optical network products into Germany, France, Spain, United Kingdom and other developed countries and regions. In October 2003, Huawei won the CDMA450[3] project contract with the European telecom operator Inquam, entering the CDMA450 mobile system market in Portugal, Germany, Romania, Russia, and Sweden. Inquam's CFO said that the key to their choice of the company was "Huawei's vitality and strong R&D capabilities."

In 2004, Huawei set up its European regional headquarters in the United Kingdom, shifting focus from developing countries to Europe's mainstream high-end markets. Finally, in 2005, Huawei became an equipment supplier to British Telecom. In November 2005, Huawei signed a global procurement framework agreement with Vodafone, the world's largest mobile communications operator, and starting in 2006, Huawei provided customized mobile phones for 21 countries operated by Vodafone. Using this as a springboard, Huawei quickly opened up the European mobile phone market using a "carrier network and customized mobile phone" model, and laid a solid foundation for the future entry of Huawei high-end mobile phones into Europe.

In 2016, Huawei's sales revenue in Europe reached RMB 156.5 billion, accounting for 30% of total revenue and making it Huawei's biggest overseas market. According to data from GfK[4], in 2016, Huawei's mobile phones had a market share of more than 15% in 33 countries, and a market share of more than 20% in a further 18 countries, of which nearly half were European. Both in the carrier business and in the mobile phone business, Huawei has achieved good results in Europe, offering local telecom operators good-value products and services. Huawei believes that cost-effective products and the ability to respond quickly to customer needs are among the main reasons that Huawei has repeatedly obtained orders from overseas operators.

---

3   A CDMA2000 cellular system that operates in the 450-470 MHz frequency band rather than the 900, 1,800 and 2,100 MHz ranges. CDMA450 reduces the number of cells in a network because the lower frequency transmits longer distances. As of January 2009, approximately one hundred cellular carriers offered CDMA450 in 51 countries around the world except in North America and Australia

4   GfK (Growth from Knowledge) is an international market data and research company.

Huawei's expansion into the U.S. market

The U.S. was identified by Ren Zhengfei as the one truly global mainstream market. A breakthrough in the U.S. market would be of decisive significance compared to other regional markets. First of all, the U.S. is the world's largest telecommunications equipment market and second, in the U.S. market, Huawei faces full-scale pressure from Cisco and other telecommunications equipment giants. Third, unlike the decentralized European telecom equipment market, the U.S. is the largest single market in the world and is strictly regulated by the government. Overcoming political resistance is the key problem foreign companies must overcome. In such a market and in the process of confronting its competitors, Huawei is not only restricted by high technical barriers to entry but is also subject to political factors and trade protection bans.

Early phase strategy: Fighting alone (1999-2003)

Early in 1999, Huawei set up a research institute in Dallas dedicated to developing products for the American market, and in June 2001, Huawei established a wholly-owned subsidiary – Futurewei Technologies – in Texas, selling broadband and data products to local businesses. Just as in the European market, Huawei's advantage in the U.S. was cost effectiveness.

But Huawei's advances in the U.S. market were accompanied by market doubts about its products. At the beginning of 2003, Cisco sued Huawei in the Texas State Court for violating its intellectual property. After a year and a half of patent disputes, the two sides finally reached a settlement, but the dispute seriously affected Huawei's reputation, slowing down business development in the American market.

Medium-term: Joint-venture strategy (2003-2007)

A joint venture founded by Huawei and 3Com played a critical role in the patent dispute with Cisco, and helped Huawei directly appreciate the significance of alliance strategies. Huawei then began to explore the international market by way of joint-venture models. It sought opportunities for cooperation with the four major U.S. operators (Verizon, ATT, Sprint, and T-Mobile) by linking up with other counterparts. In November 2003, Huawei's joint venture with 3Com, "Huawei 3Com Communication Technology Co., Ltd. (H3C)," was formally established with Huawei investing technology and personnel for a 51% stake, while 3Com invested US$160 million for a 49% stake. According to the agreement, data products were sold under the joint venture brand in China and Japan, while in other markets they were sold under the 3Com brand. For Huawei, this global joint venture was strategically important. With the help of 3Com's brand and global distribution channels, Huawei could offer OEM products at competitive prices through nearly 50,000 3Com distribution points around the world, thus also indirectly providing an entry point to the U.S. Also in 2007, Huawei and U.S. mobile operator LeapWireless reached agreement on a first cooperation.

Huawei had finally made some progress in the U.S. carrier market. But Huawei's business was mainly providing services to small and medium-sized operators, and it had yet to sign a contract with one of the four major mobile operators that dominate the U.S. market. Huawei's strategy of opening up the U.S. market through joint ventures also had little success.

Latter phase: Acquisition strategy (2008-2012)

After 2008, Huawei tried to enter the U.S. through mergers and acquisitions, but it was repeatedly blocked.

On February 25, 2011, Huawei's Vice Chairman Hu Houkun published an open letter on the company's website to clarify long-standing inaccurate rumors and invited the U.S. authorities to conduct a formal investigation of Huawei. Using this as an opportunity, the U.S. Congress launched an 18-month investigation into Huawei and ZTE. The U.S. House Intelligence Committee issued a report in 2012 saying that Huawei and ZTE's products threatened U.S. national security and warned U.S. telecommunications companies not to purchase their equipment.

During this period, the U.S. government and CFIUS gave Huawei almost no opportunities for direct access to the U.S. market. The problems facing Huawei were acute and obvious. After more than ten years of development, Huawei's operating revenues in the U.S. market had increased from US$40 million in 2006 to US$1.3 billion in 2011 (of which approximately US$1.2 billion came from sales of smart phones, tablet PCs, and other devices). But in the context of Huawei's total revenues of RMB 203.9 billion, this was still very poor.

Table 1: Huawei Blocked in the U.S.

Three acquisitions vetoed	1.	In 2008, Huawei and Bain Capital attempted to buy 3Com. The deal was vetoed by the Committee on Foreign Investment in the United States (CFIUS)
	2.	In 2010, Huawei tried to buy Motorola's wireless assets, a deal also rejected by the U.S. government
	3.	In 2010, Huawei tried to acquire 2Wire, a broadband network software vendor but failed because 2Wire was afraid that the acquisition would not be approved
One patent acquisition vetoed	1.	In 2010, Huawei tried to buy 3Leaf's patented technology for $2 million, but the deal was considered "a threat to U.S. security" by CFIUS. Huawei finally canceled the deal in February 2011
Two contracts vetoed	1.	In 2009, AT&T 4G equipment contract was vetoed by the U.S. National Security Agency (NSA)
	2.	In 2010, Sprint4G equipment contract was vetoed by the U.S. Department of Commerce

Source: CKGSB Case Center

Two Huawei M&A failures in the U.S.

Case 1: Huawei and 3Com Corporation

There were two reasons for a Huawei acquisition of 3Com, the first of which was Huawei's need for a globalization strategy. After several years of global exploration, Huawei discovered that it was difficult and costly to establish its own brand in developed markets such as Europe and the U.S. As a modern network communication technology company, 3Com had good sales channels and a large customer base, and through its acquisition, Huawei could quickly enter the U.S. market in a strategic way and increase its market share.

The second was Huawei's need for strategic transformation. In order to adapt to the revolutionary changes that were taking place in the telecommunications industry, Huawei began to expand its business from telecom operating networks to the corporate and consumer sectors.

Huawei's focus had long been on the operator market, and following its complete withdrawal from H3C[5], it clearly recognized the importance of the enterprise market. The acquisition of 3Com could make up for Huawei's lack of segmentation in the corporate networks market.

Established in 1979, 3Com was one of the founders of modern network telecommunications technology. Its founder, Bob Metcalfe, is the inventor of Ethernet technology. In 1998, 3Com had global sales of US$5.4 billion, second only to Cisco's US$8.5 billion, and it was Cisco's main competitor.

In 1999, due to the impact of the Internet bubble, 3Com's profitability fell and resulted in the company's performance reporting a loss. In 2000, 3Com lost its technological advantage in the high-end enterprise network equipment market and eventually withdrew from that market to focus primarily on faster-growing businesses such as the consumer network business. By 2002, 3Com had conducted large-scale global layoffs and shifted its focus to the China market.

On the eve of the acquisition, 3Com, after becoming the sole owner of H3C, found itself in financial distress. According to financial data disclosed on September 20, 3Com's sales in the first quarter of fiscal year 2008 were only US$319 million and its losses totaled US$18.7 million. Meanwhile, more than 30% of revenue and 95% of profits came from H3C, while H3Cs revenue came mainly from Huawei. 3Com's operations were unsustainable.

On September 28, 2007, Huawei teamed up with Bain Capital and announced a US$2.2 billion bid for 3Com. Bain Capital would hold 83.5% of 3Com's shares, and Huawei 16.5%, with an all-cash payment of $363 million being made via its wholly-owned subsidiary in Hong Kong. Huawei also reserved the right to increase its share by a further 5% in the future. Initially, 3Com agreed to the deal but six months later CFIUS[6] blocked it on the grounds that it was a threat to the U.S. government's information security. Bain was forced to back out and the deal was aborted. On November 12, 2009, 3Com was bought by Hewlett-Packard for $2.7 billion.

---

5   H3C was a joint venture established by Huawei and 3Com in 2003 with Huawei holding 51% of the shares and 3Com 49%. In November 2005, Huawei transferred 2% of the equity of the joint venture company to 3Com at a price of US$28 million, giving 3Com a 51% controlling share. On November 15, 2006, 3Com initiated the bidding process and on November 29, Huawei accepted the bid and temporarily abandoned H3C. 3Com finally acquired the 49% of the shares held by Huawei for US$882 million, and gained full ownership of H3C.

6   The Committee on Foreign Investment in the United States is an inter-agency committee of the United States Government that reviews the national security implications of foreign investments in U.S. companies or operations. Chaired by the United States Secretary of the Treasury, CFIUS includes representatives from 16 U.S. departments and agencies, including the Defense, State and Commerce departments, as well as (most recently) the Department of Homeland Security.

The rise in U.S. trade protectionism and the "China threat" theory were the main reasons for the failure of these M&A attempts. As a veteran telecommunications equipment company, 3Com had been providing computer anti-intrusion inspection equipment to the Pentagon, the U.S. Army and intelligence agencies, and concerns over threats to these critical computer networks prompted the U.S. government to block the acquisitions. Meanwhile, the background of Huawei's leader, Ren Zhengfei, a retired Chinese military veteran, exacerbated concerns among U.S. regulatory authorities. Furthermore, Huawei's opaque management presented problems for regulators. As a fully independent, privately-owned company (the only non-listed company on the Fortune Global 500 list), Huawei's long-term approach of being deliberately low-key, refusing to disclose its detailed shareholder structure and evading the media has made it difficult for the U.S. government to understand it.

Third, the way Huawei structured the 3Com deal also raised concerns for U.S. government regulators. After the acquisition, Huawei held only 16.5% of H3C shares, but in fact Huawei actually maintained a very close relationship with H3C both in terms of personnel and business. For example, most H3C employees and 30% of its sales revenue came from Huawei. As a result, U.S. regulators were concerned that after the acquisition, Huawei's influence on 3Com would exceed what was warranted from its shareholding percentage.

Case 2: Huawei acquisition of 3Leaf patents and technology

By 2011, Huawei had already built 20 cloud computing data centers. Its acquisition of 3Leaf was aimed at helping to expand its overseas business. Also, 3leaf owned cloud computing technology that Huawei wanted.

3Leaf Systems is a high-tech enterprise located in Silicon Valley, which provides server virtualization solutions for enterprise data centers. The key cloud computing technology and virtualization architecture that it had mastered could significantly improve the performance of client servers, but due to internal mismanagement, the company faced a bankruptcy crisis.

In May 2010, Huawei spent $2 million to purchase some of 3Leaf patents and to employ a dozen 3Leaf employees. According to the regulations, before the completion of a potentially sensitive cross-border acquisition, it is necessary to pro-actively apply to CFIUS for a review. Huawei and 3Leaf executives believed that the transaction involved only intellectual property purchases and employee engagement, and that 3Leaf's assets and servers were not part of the acquisition. In September 2010, Huawei applied for an opinion from the U.S. Department of Commerce regarding technology export issues involved in the acquisition, and obtained a "no permission required" ruling. But Pentagon officials then took the view that the deal was actually a corporate acquisition and needed to be reviewed. It repeatedly requested Huawei to submit to the review procedures.

In November 2010, Huawei submitted an application to CFIUS requesting that the transaction be reviewed and expressing willingness to cooperate fully. In February 2011, CFIUS informed Huawei that due to national security reasons, it proposed a cancellation of the proposed 3Leaf transaction. On February 20, 2011, Huawei withdrew its application for the acquisition of the 3Leaf patents.

While in legal terms Huawei's acquisition of 3Leaf met compliance requirements, the overall political climate in the U.S. had not improved and the upsurge in protectionism indirectly resulted in the failure of the deal. CFIUS blocked the deal in light of concerns that leakage of advanced U.S. technology after the acquisition would pose a threat to national security.

But there were also problems with Huawei's approach to this acquisition. First, a lack of communication with U.S. federal and state policy makers has led to a public debate on commercial issues in the U.S. in which Huawei is always at a disadvantage. In addition, Huawei falls short in terms of its publicity efforts with the American media and public. In U.S. media reports in the past, Huawei has always appeared in a negative light, placing it at a disadvantage in terms of public opinion.

Huawei's U.S. market strategy in transition

After having been blocked multiple times from making acquisitions in the U.S. from 2008 to 2012, Huawei reluctantly withdrew from the U.S. telecommunications equipment market. But since the U.S. market accounts for approximately 50% of the global telecommunications market, its loss meant Huawei would struggle to continue to grow in the network equipment market.

Huawei had long realized this, and in 2010 it began a process of strategic transformation and rearrangement and in addition to network devices, it opened up consumer and enterprise business lines. It began to seek new development strategies to address the U.S. market and shifted the focus of its U.S. business from telecommunications equipment to consumer products. It also started paying more attention to R&D and patent protection of intellectual property, to try to break through technical constraints in terms of competitors and to reduce patent disputes.

In 2015, Huawei mobile phones began to make some progress in the U.S. Huawei started working with Google and produced the Nexus 6P smartphone, then tried to break into the sales channels of the four major U.S. carriers through mobile phone OEM arrangements. In 2016, Huawei cooperated with Microsoft and Intel to launch the Matebook laptop computer in the U.S., and gained entry to Microsoft's flagship stores.

But Huawei is currently still marginalized in the U.S. Huawei and the four major U.S. operators, which account for 80-90% of the mobile phone market, have no point of intersection. Unable to sell telecommunications equipment into the U.S. market, Huawei cannot simply replicate the strategy of "bundling mobile phones with operators" that it adopted in the European market. And in the absence of support from the operators, Huawei has difficulty gaining mainstream visibility for its smartphones with American consumers. The main sales website launched by Huawei, GetHuawei.com, does not seem to get much traffic and according to data from market research firm Canalys, Huawei's U.S. market share in the third quarter of 2016 was only 0.4%, compared with Apple's 39% and Samsung's 23%.

Huawei's American dream

For any equipment manufacturer in the telecommunications industry, the U.S. market cannot be ignored. Mobile telecommunications originated in the U.S., and the U.S. has the most powerful innovation capability and also the world's most stringent telecommunications regulatory standards. At the same time, the U.S. is the world's strongest economy, with a large number of users and strong spending power. In a sense, product acceptance by the U.S. market means acceptance by the world.

For Huawei, the American dream has taken it on a long and difficult journey. This is not only a problem at the enterprise level, regarding technology and capabilities, culture and communication. It has also affected industry-wide and political arenas. The telecommunications industry is often intertwined with national security, and the obstructions from the U.S.

government are a unique feature of this insurmountable industry. For many U.S. consumers, Huawei is already a familiar name, but it will take a very long time for Huawei to be truly understood and accepted.

Despite all its setbacks, Huawei is still trying to get into the U.S. through various routes, and Ren Zhengfei still has great hopes particularly for Huawei mobile phones in that market. "Huawei as a whole can only break through the U.S. blockade if its frontline is sharpened," he said in an internal speech. "Otherwise, it will pull down the company's capabilities to a mediocre level and no walls will be breached."

Where will Huawei's "sharp frontline" be, and when will Huawei's American dream be realized? This is in fact not only Huawei's American dream, but also the American dream of all Chinese companies.

8. Midea's Takeover of KUKA

A New Milestone for Overseas M&A

Supervising Professor: Jennifer Huang; Case Researcher: Di Deng

In the 2002 James Bond action movie, Die Another Day, lead actress Halle Berry found herself fighting laser-welding robots in a gigantic ice palace. The firm that made the robots, KUKA, was to make global headlines for a second time on May 18, 2016, when China's Midea Group offered to pay €115 per share in a daring takeover bid. The news hit Europe like a bombshell. Midea was completely unknown in KUKA's home country, Germany. One report summed up the sentiment: "Previously, German companies acquired by China were distressed ones, the latest is a successful German company, and, what's more, a cutting-edge high-tech company."[1] Valued at €4.5 billion, this would be one of the biggest international M&As ever carried out by a Chinese company, with huge implications for the robotics and home appliances sectors in China and globally.

Industrial Robotics

China's rapidly aging population and rising labor costs have given rise to a great potential demand for robots. Indeed, since 2013, China has been home to the world's largest market for robots, even though utilization rates are still far below those of developed countries.

Robots comprise of two main types: service and industrial[2]. Service robots

---

1   Frankfurter Journal.
2   International Federation of Robotics (IFR).

may be used to provide medical care, home entertainment or housekeeping. Industrial robots undertake functions such as handling, stacking, welding, painting and industrial production assembly, bringing manufacturing closer to automation. They are highly stable and efficient, and are suited to high-risk environments. KUKA robots are concentrated in the industrial robot category.

An industrial robot consists primarily of a body, servo motors, reducers, controllers and sensors, and the industrial robot manufacturing chain can be divided into three parts: upstream (three core components: servo motors, reducers and controllers), midstream (body), and downstream (system integration). Due to the high degree of difficulty in the technical development of the upstream core components, the corresponding costs are also high.[3]

Four robotics giants – FANUC, Yaskawa, KUKA, and ABB – account for about half of the global robotics market, and in 2015, their shares of the global market were 17%, 11%, 9% and 9% respectively.

From a margins perspective, the further upstream a core technology or product is, the better its profit margin. FANUC develops its own upstream core components such as control and drive system products and ranks first in profitability. Ranking last, with its concentration in the midstream and downstream, is KUKA.

Midea's Tough Transformation

When He Xiangjian organized a group of villagers to start producing plastic bottle caps in 1968, he could never have envisioned that 49 years later, his small workshop would turn into one of the biggest home appliance makers in China, and would be bidding to take over a major player in industrial robotics.

Starting from bottle caps, with no technological element or bright prospects, Midea tried many different products, and in 1981, entered the home appliance sector via electric fans. By July 2017, with US$24.06 billion in annual revenues, Midea made it to 450 on the Fortune 500 list, the first

---

3   The cost proportions of industrial robots are probably 22% for the main body, 25% for the servo system, 38% for the speed reducers, 10% for the control system and 5% for other systems. Of the core components, the gross margin of the reducers is the highest at 40%, while the gross margin of servo motors and controllers range from around 20% to 30%, from In-depth Report on Industrial Robots: China Becomes a New Engine for the Growth. 767stock.com, https://baijiahao.baidu.com/s?id=1559203 266962457&wfr=spider&for=pc, 2017-02-13.

Figure 1: Density of Industrial Robots

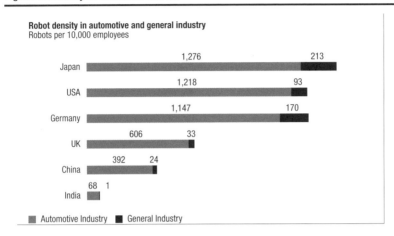

Robot density in automotive and general industry
Robots per 10,000 employees

Japan — 1,276 / 213
USA — 1,218 / 93
Germany — 1,147 / 170
UK — 606 / 33
China — 392 / 24
India — 68 / 1

■ Automotive Industry ■ General Industry

Source: Annual Report of KUKA in 2016

Chinese home appliance firm to appear on the list.

The home appliance industry had grown in line with China's booming economy, and had helped boost the sales revenues of all three of the top home appliance companies in China – Midea, Gree Electric, and Haier – to the RMB 100 billion level. Growth had targeted scale rather than efficiency, however, and meant large debts were necessary to fund expansion. In 2012, He Xiangjian, the founder, stepped aside for his prodigé Paul Fang. Along with the change in leadership, Midea rolled out a stock options scheme for staff, and outside of He Xiangjian's family, Paul Fang became the biggest shareholder. Yet, even before the founder's resignation, Paul Fang had led the management team to implement sweeping reforms. Although Midea had made more than RMB 100 billion in 2010, he was worried.

Paul Fang guided Midea Group through a difficult transformation from scale-based to efficiency-based development. In the next five years, Midea closed more than ten production bases, eliminated many low-margin products and halved staff numbers to under 100,000. In 2012, Midea's sales revenues plummeted by RMB 30 billion, but after a temporary but painful transition, Midea Group's revenues and profitability grew steadily.

Midea has on many occasions leveraged capital to facilitate vertical and horizontal integration and acquisitions, to acquire core technologies, to enrich product categories and to open up market channels. In 1998, Midea purchased Macro from Toshiba, becoming the only producer in China with air conditioning compressor technology. Midea then bought a magnetron plant from Sanyo for its core microwave oven technology, and two local brands, Royalstar in 2004 and Cygnet in 2008, to extend its business to refrigerators and washing machines. As the domestic market became saturated, Midea turned its attention to foreign markets and picked up speed with overseas acquisitions. In 2016 alone, Midea launched three major transnational acquisitions worth over RMB 30 billion, for 80.1% of shares in Toshiba's white goods business, 80% of shares in Clivet, an Italian central air conditioning brand, and 94.55% of KUKA.

The acquisition of KUKA was justified in these words, "Midea may use KUKA's technological advantages in the fields of industrial robots and automated production to increase the company's production efficiency and promote its manufacturing upgrade."

Made in China 2025?

Midea's offer to purchase KUKA in 2016 highlighted the company's strategic shift towards smart manufacturing. It was also symbolic of China's white goods sector's search for a transformational breakthrough.

The domestic market was almost completely saturated and new opportunities involved either overseas expansion or a breakthrough in scale at home by shifting to smart home appliances. The dilemma faced by home appliance producers reflected the overall predicament of China's manufacturing industries. A report by Boston Consulting Group indicates that China's manufacturing costs are already close to those in the U.S. (ratio of manufacturing costs: 0.96:1). In addition, the re-industrialization and high-end manufacturing strategy of developed countries and rapidly-expanding assembly lines in Latin America and Southeast Asia were squeezing China. The big trends were from low-end to high-end, and from low-cost and large-scale to high-tech automation. National policies and initiatives such as "Made in China 2025" pivoted domestic companies' orientation to transition and upgrade.

Haier, Gree and Midea all turned towards "overseas development" and "smart manufacturing," but followed very distinctive paths.

Haier has emphasized Internet innovation and a focus on customers. CEO Zhang Ruimin has talked of reshaping the value chain around the user and transform Haier from a "traditional manufacturing enterprise of home appliances" into a "platform for incubating entrepreneurs on behalf of society as a whole," and to provide users with smart home solutions using the Internet. The C2M (customer to manufacturer) model adopted by Haier's Internet-based factories highlights the user's experience and connections to the production process.

Haier acquired GE Appliances at a price of US$5.58 billion, beating out Midea and Electrolux, gaining control of its global logistics and retail network. This acquisition of GE Appliances boosted its market share in the U.S. to 20%. Haier then had six brands, from high-end GE Appliances and Casa Imperial to mid-range Haier and on to the Tongshuai brand aimed at young users. In all, Haier covered 160 countries worldwide, with 108 manufacturing plants (54 of them overseas) and ten R&D centers. According to Haier's financial report, GE Appliances contributed sales revenue of RMB 25.834 billion and a net profit of RMB 435 million from June 7, 2016 to the end of 2016.

In contrast to Haier's "Internet Thinking," Gree and Midea have invested in robotics to improve manufacturing. "All our robots and core technologies are independently researched and developed," said Dong Mingzhu, Gree Electric's Chairwoman. "I have no comment on the costly acquisitions of other companies." Gree prefers to develop core technologies independently in transitioning from being a pure home appliance manufacturer towards new energy industries and equipment manufacturing. Its R&D focuses on two key fields, robotics and precision machining tools, and Gree has independently mastered the whole span of robotics research, development and production, including components' production, assembly and downstream applications. Since 2013, its self-developed robots and other smart equipment have also been sold externally on a small scale, and by the end of 2016, sales topped RMB 1 billion. But researchers at Gree admitted there was still a gap between their proprietary robots and those of KUKA and ABB in terms of positional accuracy, stability, design and control structure.

After failing to acquire GE Appliances, Midea moved to buy brands in Japan and Europe. In 2016, the company paid RMB 3.2 billion for the home appliance business of Toshiba, and while that brought with it the Japanese market and advanced products and technologies, it lost Midea RMB 188 million by the first quarter of 2017. The challenge Midea faced was how to successfully integrate and re-invigorate this established but loss-making brand. Additionally, Midea purchased 80% of the equity of Clivet (an Italian central air-conditioning brand) and at about the same time announced its tender offer for KUKA.

Targets of acquisition

R&D strength in China's domestic robotics industry is fairly weak. 75% of the more than 4,000 robot makers in China are downstream system integrators, for which quality and reliability tends to be low.[4] No more than ten companies make upstream core components, midstream robots and downstream system integration services. Additionally, leading companies such as SISUN[5] and GSK[6] have high valuations and, hence, are not the most attractive investment targets.

Yaskawa had a similar market value and global market share to Midea and was already a supplier of robots to Midea's factories. In August 2015, Midea and Yaskawa launched their strategic cooperation, investing RMB 200 million to establish Guangdong Yaskawa-Midea Industrial Robot Co., Ltd. ("Yaskawa-Midea") and Guangdong Midea-Yaskawa Service Robot Co., Ltd. ("Midea-Yaskawa"). In 2016, Yaskawa held 51% shares of Yaskawa-Midea, which went into operation in March that year, mainly manufacturing robot bodies and system integration appliances to meet the automation requirements of Midea's plants. As of February 2017, Yaskawa had received orders worth over RMB 80 million, 60% of which came from Midea and the rest from other 3C (computers, consumer electronics, and communications) appliance companies. According to the joint venture company, it was still in R&D and pilot phase in 2017, the actual use of robots was relatively limited and an expansion to market scale would still take some time. This is because the home appliance industry has a shorter cycle with more products than the automobile manufacturing industry, involving a higher-level production process and higher requirements for robot bodies and components.

Midea holds a 61% share of Midea-Yaskawa, which focuses on medical robotics' R&D, with Yaskawa providing the technology and Midea primarily contributing operations and marketing input. It is understood that the joint venture is currently developing robots for the rehabilitation, elderly care and disabled care sectors.

---

4 Industrial Control China website.
5 新松 Xinsong.
6 广数 Guangshu.

So the question is, why did Midea choose not to acquire Yaskawa? Media reports said that they might have discussed it, but did not reach agreement. When interviewed after the KUKA acquisition, the Yaskawa president said: "Our joint venture with Midea produces general-use robots. They can be used in Midea's equipment and also sold to other appliance makers. However, Midea also needs dedicated robots that are used only for its own devices. That may be one of the reasons for acquiring KUKA." He also said that the company's cooperation with Midea would not be affected by the KUKA acquisition: "Business will be the same as usual," while it may in the future also provide products to Gree and Haier[7].

Midea's approach is related more to the model of "acquisition + cooperation," and there are a number of examples, particularly in terms of the robotics industrial chain. Before purchasing KUKA, Midea acquired China's robot producer EFORT and established a joint-venture company with Japan's Yaskawa. But the takeover of KUKA was Midea's most important step in its shift towards smart manufacturing.

By 2016, Midea was the leader of the three China white goods giants with sales revenues and profit of RMB 144.4 billion and RMB 15.5 billion respectively, compared to Gree's RMB 100.7 billion and RMB 13.9 billion, and Haier's RMB 111.4 billion and RMB 6.3 billion. In terms of net profit, Gree was top with Midea second and Haier third. Midea invested the most in R&D – about RMB 6 billion – while Gree and Haier invested around RMB 4 billion and RMB 3.2 billion respectively.

KUKA

Founded in 1898, KUKA is a world-leading industrial robot producer and was viewed as being one of the stars of Germany's "Industry 4.0" revitalization initiative. KUKA was a pioneer in indoor and urban lighting and later expanded into welding tools, equipment and vehicles. In 1978, KUKA invented the world's first industrial robot, called FAMULUS.

KUKA's robots function as material handlers and welders, and are used in a wide range of industries such as automotive, aerospace, logistics, food, plastics and medicine. Especially strong in the automobile manufacturing industry,

---

7   "President of Yaskawa Talks about the Takeover of KUKA," cn.nikkei.com, http://cn.nikkei.com/columnviewpoint/viewpoint/21468-20160918.html, 2016-09-18

KUKA had the largest global market share in 2016,[8] particularly among German automobile producers such as BMW, Daimler, Mercedes-Benz and Volkswagen, where KUKA has a market share as high as 98%[9]. KUKA has Boeing, Harley, IKEA, Budweiser and Coca-Cola as robotics clients.

The company won the RedDot Award for its smooth, orange designs. Its technical strengths are also reflected in its latest small, smart robot, LBR iiwa, which can approach objects at speeds of 10mm and 50mm per second, rebound quickly when encountering obstacles, touch an egg without breaking it and touch a human hand without causing injury.

Over 100 years old, KUKA has seen several changes in its shareholder structure. In 1980, the Quandt Family took the company public and subsequently exited the company. Until the tender offer from Midea, KUKA's two largest shareholders were Voith[10] and Friedhelm Loh[11], holding 25.1% and 10% of the shares respectively. Others held less than 3%, with no

Figure 2: Income Composition of KUKA

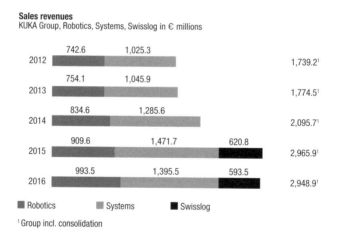

Sales revenues
KUKA Group, Robotics, Systems, Swisslog in € millions

■ Robotics　■ Systems　■ Swisslog

[1] Group incl. consolidation

Source: Annual Report of KUKA in 2016

8   IFR (International Federation of Robotics) 2015.
9   Dongwu Securities: "From Beauty to Wisdom : 1+1>2?" 2017-05-22
10 The Voith GmbH & Co. KGaA, which is headquartered in Germany, is a family-owned multinational corporation in the mechanical engineering sector with worldwide operations.
11 A German billionaire businessman. He is the founder and chairman of the Friedhelm Loh Group, a manufacturing company that grew out of a business he inherited from his father.

disclosure requirements.

KUKA made moves of its own in the capital markets. It purchased Reis, a well-known system integration service provider, in 2014, to enhance its own system integration business. In 2015, it bought Swisslog for US$335 million. The acquisition introduced mobile robotics and logistics storage businesses to KUKA, making possible integrated automatic client solutions.

Takeover: Full of twists and turns

Before making its formal offer, Midea stealthily built up its holdings of KUKA shares in three stages. In August 2015, Midea Group bought a first tranche of 5.4% of KUKA's shares in the secondary market and, soon after, signed a cooperation agreement with Yaskawa. In February 2016, Midea increased its holdings to 10.2% and then to 13.5%, becoming KUKA's second-largest shareholder. On May 18, 2016, Midea launched its bid for KUKA through MECCA, a fully-owned overseas subsidiary, offering €115 per share, raising the shareholding ratio to more than 30%. €115 was a 36% premium to the previous day's closing share price and a 60% premium to the closing price in February, before Midea raised its stake to 10.2%.

It is worth noting that the acquisition method adopted by Midea – unsolicited takeover – is rarely used. Without invitation and with no prior communication with the board and substantial shareholders, this acquisition approach is in some circumstances referred to as a hostile takeover. So when Midea announced its bid, it shocked KUKA's shareholders, the media and the government, as well as the general public. In recent years, Chinese companies have increasingly made such unsolicited acquisitions. In 2015, there were 17 such cases and in the first half of 2016, a total of 13. However, in the past five years, half of the active acquisitions by Chinese companies ended in failure.

When Midea announced its bid, many senior German and European Union officials were adamantly against it, while shareholders both large and small objected it. The acquisition raised concerns and political pressures.

First, both Germany and European Union worried that KUKA's core technologies would be pilfered by China. As one of the four giants of the robotics industry, KUKA enjoys advanced technologies and high brand value. Considered part of the "Industry 4.0" strategy, the KUKA Group is one of the core links connecting front-end advanced manufacturing companies such as BMW and Daimler and back-end data integration. KUKA's latest robots are also used to assist in Germany's "Industry 4.0" manufacturing upgrades. A member of the EU Digital Economy Committee, Gunther Oettinger, told the media, "In order to avoid the loss of key technologies, KUKA should reserve more shares for European investors."[12]

Second, KUKA is a successful German enterprise. Most German companies previously acquired by Chinese companies were either small or badly-managed, whereas KUKA was one of the best-known industrial robotics firms in the world, with broad market prospects and good operations. It was not in need of a large infusion of capital.

But KUKA's management did not indicate opposition to the takeover, and on May 28, KUKA's CEO, Till Reuter, welcomed the offer saying: "I absolutely do not see this as a hostile takeover."[13] Reuter said that KUKA was already a robot supplier to Midea and that the two companies had been in discussion for several weeks about how to improve shared logistics and service robots, as well as how to jointly conduct market promotions.[14]

However, it appeared that KUKA's major shareholders had not been informed before the bid was announced. The CEO of the largest shareholder, Voith, came out publically against the acquisition. As the largest shareholder, Voith had the power to veto any management proposal in a shareholders' meeting.

On the face of it, there was no way the German government could block the acquisition. Nevertheless, the Minister of Economic Affairs Sigmar Gabriel publicly called on shareholders not to sell shares to Midea Group and on several occasions tried to find German and other European companies to purchase KUKA. The German government contacted several companies, such as ABB and Siemens, but all declined the opportunity.

In the face of huge pressure from the government and public opinion, Midea actively sought the support of KUKA's management and also referenced previously successful acquisitions made by Chinese companies to assuage concerns. Paul Fang sent out a stream of positive signals, saying that KUKA would remain independent and that there was no intention to de-list it from the stock market. He also publicly expressed respect for the local

12 Why has the takeover of KUKA concerned Germany so much? China Business Journal. http://www. cb.com.cn/companies/2016_0616/1165392.html, 20160616

13 Why the Takeover of KUKA concerns German so much? China Business Journal. http://www.cb.com.cn/ companies/2016_0616/1165392.html, 20160616

14 "Verbal Intervention" of German Government May be Blocked. Wallstreetcn.com, https://wallstreetcn. com/articles/246410, 2016-06-01

culture, for the local management team and for the independence of KUKA.

Furthermore, during Chancellor Merkel's trip to China in early June 2016, Premier Li Keqiang raised the issue and expressed the view that Midea's acquisition was in line with market economics and that "both China and Germany should show a supportive and open attitude towards mutual cooperation between enterprises implemented according to market principles and international practices within the legal framework." Following non-public communications and agreements between the two governments, the German side acquiesced.

Setting aside the impact of public opinion and political influence, two factors probably account for the success of Midea's acquisition of KUKA: first, winning the support of KUKA's management and shareholders by making the commitment to maintain management independence and, second, offering a high price to shareholders.

On June 16, 2016, as an expression of sincerity, Midea gave five assurances to KUKA, namely: no plant closures, no staff cuts, trade secrets protected, no control of the company and no de-listing from the stock market. This maintained the independence of management, provided support for KUKA's

Table 1: The Process of Midea's Acquisition of KUKA

On August 21, 2015, 5.43% shares; and on February 3, 2016, 10.22% shares.				
May 18, 2016 – tender offer announced	June 16, 2016 – tender offer officially launched	August 3, 2016 – offer period ends	December 30, 2016 – all conditions of acquisition met	January 6, 2017 – deal completed
Midea tender offer at a price of €115 / share was proposed; Intention to increase its holdings to over 30%	On June 6, the offer was approved by a Midea shareholders' meeting; On June 15, it was approved by Federal Financial Authority	81.04% of the shares accepted the offer	30% minimum acceptance threshold approved by regulatory agencies of various countries (7+1)	Payment made of total acquisition amount of €3.7 billion; Officially holds 94.55% of KUKA Group shares

Source: Midea's disclosed information

efforts to open up the China market and provided funds for R&D. KUKA's management team, the board of directors and the supervisory board all expressed satisfaction with this. On June 28, 2016, Midea and the KUKA group formally signed the "investment agreement," with an effective period of seven and a half years from the date of signature.

As a German company, KUKA has a dual-level governance structure consisting of an executive board and a supervisory board. The executive board is composed of senior executives responsible for daily operations. The supervisory board consists of shareholders and staff representatives, 50% each, and is responsible for appointing and supervising the executive board. The supervisory board cannot intervene in daily affairs, but has the right to oversee major transactions. According to documents publicly released by KUKA, its executive board operates independently with its personnel structure unchanged following the acquisition. Midea attends the board of supervisors as a shareholder representative. According to the shareholding ratio, Midea will arrange six representatives to be on the KUKA supervisory board. In addition, in accordance with the German Corporate Governance

Figure 3: Details of Mutual Agreement

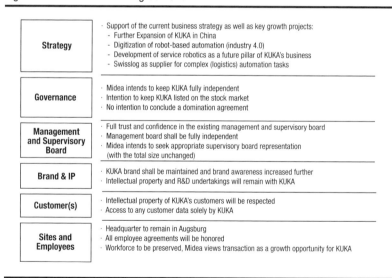

Source: Public Data from Midea and KUKA

Act, there will be an additional number of independent expert representatives sitting on the board of supervisors.

The agreement providing a commitment to KUKA's independence, together with the support of management and employees and the high offer price, quickly changed the attitude of major shareholders. At that time, the two largest shareholders were Voith and Loh, which held 25.1% and 10% of the shares respectively. The remaining institutional and individual shareholders all held less than 3% of shares, obviating the need for disclosure. Given Midea's offer of €115, well above KUKA's share price, and the five-point commitment, Voith's attitude began to soften. The share sale was in fact a very good deal for Voith, which at the time was operating at a loss. In 2014, Voith spent about €370 million to acquire 25.1% of KUKA's shares. According to Midea's offer, Voith could receive €1.2 billion, equivalent to gaining a two-year net profit of €800 million. After Voith agreed to sell its shares, the other large shareholder, German financier Loh, said he was willing to sell all his shares as well. With the "collapse" of the major shareholders, the small shareholders were also open to "persuasion." On August 3, 2016, shareholders holding 81.04% of KUKA shares accepted the proposed acquisition. Coupled with the KUKA stock already held by Midea, the company had a total KUKA stake of 94.55%.

Overpriced?

Midea's offer price of €115 per share was a premium of 36.24% over the previous day's closing share price (May 17, 2016). Acceptance of the tender offer for about 81.04% of the shares was valued at €3.71 billion, equivalent to about RMB 29.2 billion, and delivery was completed on January 6, 2017. The capital for the acquisition came from Midea Group's own funds and from syndicated loans. Midea's annual report showed that in 2015, it had a net profit of RMB 12.707 billion and cash holdings of RMB 11.86 billion. Public information shows that both ICBC (Europe) Co., Ltd. Paris Branch and ICBC Frankfurt Branch co-signed a financing agreement with MECCA, Midea's fully-owned overseas subsidiary. The financing sum was not disclosed.

In the face of criticism over the purchase price, Paul Fang said that time would resolve the valuation issue, which should be viewed from a three to five-year perspective. Gu Yanmin, Midea Group VP, also said that Midea's many years of experience in industrial chain integration was the key factor behind the KUKA acquisition. He said that the acquisition was made after

Table 2: Comparable overseas–listed companies*

Serial No.	Listed companies in the same industry	Market value (100 million RMB)	P/E	Enterprise value / EBITDA (in the last 12 months)	Enterprise value/ sales revenue (in the last 12 months)
1	ABB	2,905.4	22.9x	10.8x	1.4x
2	FANUC	1,994.3	16.1x	10.3x	3.9x
3	YASKAWA	204.2	13.8x	7.6x	0.9x
Mean			**17.6x**	**9.6x**	**2.1x**
4	KUKA	302.4	60.4x	18.2x	1.6x

Source: Wind, Report on Tender Offer of Midea's Acquisition of KUKA

Table 3: Comparable Chinese–listed companies*

Serial No.	Listed companies in the same industry	Market value (RMB 100 million)	P/E	Enterprise value / EBITDA (in the last 12 months)	Enterprise value /sales revenue (in the last 12 months)
1	Robot	379.1	95.4x	71.2x	21.4x
2	Estun	67.2	131.5x	93.4x	14.0x
3	Boshi Shares	117.8	85.7x	54.1x	16.7x
4	SanFeng Intelligent	64.2	302.9x	201.7x	18.7x
5	Yawei Machine	51.4	72.1x	43.0x	5.3x
Mean			**137.5x**	**92.68**	**15.22x**
6	KUKA	302.4	60.4x	18.2x	1.6x

Source: Wind, Report on the Tender Offer of Midea's acquisition of KUKA

* Both market value and PE were based on May 19, 2016 data; 2. The equity value as part of enterprise value was calculated with the closing price of May 19, 2016, as well as the earnings data of March 31, 2016; 3. Both EBITDA and revenue were based on the twelve months to March 31, 2016.

* 1. Both market value and PE were calculated as of May 19, 2016. 2. The equity value as part of enterprise value was calculated on the basis of the closing price on May 19, 2016, as well as earnings data in the March 31, 2016 financial report. 3. EBITDA and revenue were based on 2015 data.

a full investigation and personal participation, and that Midea would not "waste money."[15]

M&A Expectations

Midea benefits

For Midea, the acquisition of KUKA was significant in three ways.

First, the most direct benefit of buying KUKA was that it helped raise the automation level of Midea's production lines and logistics storage capabilities. The average level of automation of Midea's production lines is currently at about 17% with nearly 1,000 robots in operation – the highest level of automation in the Chinese home appliance industry. But there is still much room for improvement in terms of Midea's vision of smart automated factories devoid of staff. Stefan Lampa, the chairman of the board of management of KUKA Robot Co. Ltd. under KUKA Group, said to the media, "KUKA will help optimize Midea's assembly plants and production sites, as well as improve its warehouse logistics system. Midea hopes to update its production lines in China using KUKA's technology, and KUKA hopes to significantly increase its sales in China by cooperating with Midea, which would appear to be a win-win deal."[16]

This may also be accompanied by internal training by Midea of technical personnel and technological transfers. The use of industrial robots requires support from a great number of engineers, but such training in China is extremely inadequate. KUKA has long been involved in training in the industry and this knowledge transfer is expected to be further strengthened after KUKA becomes a part of Midea. Lampa also stated that KUKA is making more manipulable robots in order to adapt to China's specific market needs and personnel capabilities.

Additionally, the acquisition of KUKA also meant that Midea merged with the KUKA subsidiary, Swisslog Logistics, a logistics company primarily

---

15 Midea first displayed KUKA Robot to compete with Gree, baijiahao, https://baijiahao.baidu.com/s?id=1 561364878269164&wfr=spider&for=pc, 2017-03-09

16 An interview with KUKA robot's CEO Stefan Lampa: "KUKA strategy will not affected by Midea's acquisition," NetEase Finance, http://money.163.com/16/0614/00/BPFSBFP500253B0H.html, 2016-07-15

providing logistics automation solutions for hospitals, warehouses and distribution centers. In the future, it may also be integrated with Midea's Annto Logistics.

Second, following the KUKA acquisition, Midea will open up a second track in addition to home appliances – robotics. With the home appliance industry hitting growth limits, growth has slowed in Midea's main business and it faces the risk of being replaced or undercut. This is partly due to the impact of Internet companies, such as Xiaomi, extending into the smart home market and also relates to the possibility that the smart home will subvert the entire existing home appliance business model. The robotics business can help to offset the risks faced by the core business, while improving Midea's efficiency and reducing its labor costs. In its own announcement, the company stated: "Investment in robots enhances the automation of Midea's production and logistics, and also allows for R&D into robotics-based smart home devices."

The most direct approach for Midea to the robot business was through KUKA's industrial robot business, especially in terms of usage in the automobile and home appliance industries. In China, the relationship between robot suppliers and automotive OEMs is very strong and often stays unchanged for decades. Thus, KUKA's acquisition by Midea is unlikely to affect cooperation between KUKA and its clients. But KUKA's advantages in the automobile industry can be exploited by Midea. Paul Fang once declared that "in addition to Japanese cars and Tesla, robot supply for other automobile enterprises will be mostly held by us." Midea is a major player in the home appliance industry, and if future R&D is successful, robots developed by KUKA for Midea could be a way to help KUKA to enter other industries, such as home appliances and the 3C market.

Furthermore, both sides will work together to develop service robots. According to media reports, products that Midea and KUKA have started to jointly develop include a robot vacuum cleaner, as well as medical care service robots for the elderly. IFR statistics show that in 2015, sales of service robots in China increased by 16%, and the market size was about US$2.2 billion. According to market intelligence firm Tractica, the total market for service robots (including toys and vacuum cleaners) will climb to US$13.2 billion by 2022. Despite this rapid growth, the overall business model and consumer habits are not yet mature. Midea wants to further expand the service robot market in order to reduce corresponding costs and promote the popularization of such products.[17]

Third, through the vertical integration of all its acquired assets, Midea may be able to take on the role of solution provider for Germany's "Industry 4.0" plan. In the upper reaches of the robot process, Midea acquired the Israeli company Gotron, which is strong in the production of servo drivers, a core robot component and one which is complementary to KUKA's robotics. In the midstream and downstream of robotics, there are KUKA and Anhui Effort, both engaged in R&D, manufacturing and downstream integration. In addition, Midea and Yaskawa have conducted strategic cooperation on the development of robots. Therefore, Midea basically has the entire industrial chain of the robotics industry covered. In addition, Midea itself has accumulated much experience on the digital transformation and automation upgrade of its own traditional factories, and has become a model for smart factory transformation. As China's manufacturing industry explores routes towards smart manufacturing, Midea may also serve as a model and a consultant, as well as a service provider for other enterprises upgrading their factories.

Midea Group's Vice President Gu Yanmin said: "Our hope is that the final result is the integration of Midea, KUKA and Gotron's resources to create a complete enterprise-level solution. As such, KUKA would mainly be engaged in robots and some system solutions. Midea's main advantage would be in the information transformation of enterprises, especially in logistics. That coupled with Gotron's drives and motors creates a range which is vertically integrated." Such services are currently offered by industry giants such as Siemens and GE. Maybe Midea can aspire to take a share of that market.

However, at least during the seven and a half years stipulated in the agreement, it will be difficult for Midea to directly obtain KUKA's core robotics technology. KUKA retains its independence of operations and core intellectual property and R&D must stay with KUKA. Without directly criticizing Midea, Liu Shuwei, a researcher at the Central University of Finance and Economics, has said that she believes that the purchase of KUKA could not be considered a strategic investment, and that the purchase price as a financial investment was too high, effectively raising the price level for any acquisition of robotics in the future.

There were also comments that, aside from the profit distribution issue, Midea's immediate goal was to occupy the strategic high ground and lock

---

17 Bloomberg News, reprinted on Ofweek Robot, http://robot.ofweek.com/2017-04/ART-8321202-8420-30128416_4.html, 2017-04-26

in the key technologies of the robot industry chain. Among the four largest robotics groups, KUKA had a relatively small market value and the lowest threshold for acquisition. If Midea makes a move, other companies may eye the same opportunities. The intention of Midea's various acquisitions was clearly to create an integrated upstream-midstream-downstream robotics manufacturing chain. As to why Midea raised the proportion of the acquisition from the initial 30% to an almost total buyout, some sources said that Midea Group prefers an absolute control approach in foreign acquisitions to prevent outside interference in corporate governance and decision-making.

KUKA benefits

For KUKA, the main benefit of being acquired by Midea was that KUKA could exploit China's massive robotics market. In 2015, KUKA achieved sales revenues of about €3 billion, 46% from Europe, 35% from North America and 19% from Asia-Pacific and other regions. Where is the main incremental growth space for KUKA Robot? The answer is China. "China is one of the most important markets," explained KUKA's CEO. "KUKA can only better understand the China market and develop more rapidly in China through cooperation with Chinese companies."

Despite rising labor costs and overall low level manufacturing, China still has the largest and most extensive industrial market in the world. Till Reuter of KUKA Robot expressed confidence in the China market and predicted that annual growth rates could exceed 20%, far above the 14% rate in Europe and 5-10% in the U.S.[18] KUKA said it plans to increase its sales volume in the China market from €425 million in the past fiscal year to €1 billion in 2020, aiming to become China's biggest supplier of robots.

KUKA had in fact realized the importance of the Chinese market early on. KUKA established its first production base in Shanghai in 2012 and its second in 2017. However, they cannot be considered a first-mover in the market. As early as 1997, Japan's FANUC and Shanghai Electric Group jointly established Shanghai FANUC Robot Co., Ltd., which became one of the earliest robotics multinational companies to enter the Chinese market. In 2005, ABB set up a global R&D center in Shanghai and initiated the local

18 "What is Midea's plan in the 'post-merger era'?," Xinhuanet, http://news.xinhuanet.com/tech/2017-04/11/c_1120784555.htm, 2017-04-11

mass production of robots.

In 2015, the company with the highest market share in China's industrial robot market among the four groups was Japan's FANUC, accounting for 18%, followed by KUKA (14%), Sweden's ABB (13.5%) and Japan's Yaskawa (12%).

Working with Midea can help KUKA in terms of doing trials in sectors beyond the automobile industry. With the saturation of the traditional auto manufacturing industry, the four major groups have started actively seeking opportunities in industry in general, but 3C and home appliances became the focus of the fight. ABB has been engaged in the 3C market for several years, and in 2015 Yaskawa and Midea jointly developed general industrial robots for the 3C appliance industry, while FANUC has worked actively with system integrators and distributors to explore different types of industry applications. In contrast, KUKA was late in its plans for the 3C industry. By being acquired by Midea, KUKA naturally gains access to Midea's huge market and can test its applied robots in other industries.

Among the four major groups, KUKA currently has the lowest profit margins. Compared with the other three, KUKA is relatively weak in vertical integration and particularly has to deal with high purchase costs of upstream core components, which dilutes its profits. Midea itself has a motor research department and it acquired an Israeli company called Servotronix (upstream components) and has Welling Holdings Limited[19], so it can create synergies with KUKA in terms of upstream components.

Looking to the future

Can Midea complete its transformation from a global home appliances company to a global sci-tech company through the acquisition of KUKA, thereby, leaving Gree and others behind? Can KUKA become China's biggest supplier of robots? Will this acquisition allow both sides to work together and achieve their goals?

It is not yet known whether the two sides will be able to smoothly merge and integrate their cultures. After all, China has many precedents of failure in terms of overseas mergers and acquisitions. During a meeting

---

19 Welling Holdings Limited is a listed company on the Hong Kong Stock Exchange [Stock No.: HK00382]. It specializes in R & D and manufacture of motors and drive systems. The motor products that it has developed are widely used in the field of home appliances, cleaning equipment, pumps, industrial automation and so on.

Figure 4: Market Share of Industrial Robot Enterprises in China

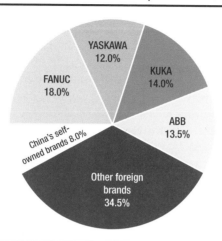

Source: China Robot Industry Alliance, marketsearch.com.cn

with investors in 2017, Midea acknowledged that integration was the biggest challenge it faced, but expressed optimism: "In this area, Midea has some empirical advantages. Midea has been expanding globally for over ten years and during that time has learned many lessons. We believe the key point is having empathy and respect for the culture of the host country." The financial results show that in 2016, KUKA's orders from China reached €530 million, an annual growth of 44%.

During an investors' meeting in the first quarter of 2017, Midea said: "We believe there is room for improvement in the profitability of KUKA and we hope to achieve this goal by giving play to synergistic factors. It has expertise in robot production and application experience in different industries, one-third in robotics and two-thirds in system integration, which can increase margins in different industry sectors. KUKA's income from China is currently about €500 million, but the potential for growth is huge. If integrated with Midea, we will assist in opening up the domestic market, establish a better ecosystem, improve market capacity and reduce costs. The results will gradually emerge next year and some specific projects will be finalized at the end of this year or early next year."

In May 2017, KUKA's CEO, Till Reuter said that in both technical and management aspects, Midea was providing KUKA with full autonomy. According to the investment agreement signed by both parties, Midea will support the independent operations of KUKA until 2023 and must not interfere in decision-making in such areas as strategy, the number of employees and the location of factories. Midea's "Hands-off Policy" temporarily allowed both sides to avoid cultural conflicts and post-investment integration problems common in cross-border mergers and acquisitions. A lawyer from Damaicheng Law Firm's Berlin branch said he believed the agreement signed by Midea and KUKA would help establish mutual trust between the two parties and help KUKA to achieve its own development as far as was possible as a subsidiary of the Midea Group.

Reuter also noted that KUKA and Midea would in future work together to develop household service robots for the consumer market, liberating people from the toil of housework. KUKA has not yet produced any service robots and currently the product it has which is closest to such a service robot is its "smart industrial operations assistant," which helps workers perform complex assembly work. "We are moving towards the consumer market, Midea is coming from another direction, and we are meeting halfway," Reuter said.

In November 2018, Till Reuter prematurely resigned from the CEO position. Dr Andy Gu, chairman of the supervisory board, thanked Reuter for his contribution to the company, adding: "Kuka is now well-positioned to re-enter a path of sustainable growth, benefiting from the increasing demand in intelligent robotics and by strengthening the position in the Chinese market."

9. Ant Micro Loan

The Social Value of Inclusive Finance

Supervising Professor: Chen Long; Case Researcher: Yang Yan[1]

Raising capital has always been difficult for small and micro-enterprises in China, but with the development of Internet technology, innovative solutions have been found. E-commerce giant Alibaba Group established two small loan companies in 2010 and 2011 to provide credit to small and micro-enterprises and individual sellers in its ecosystem. In June 2014, Ant Financial Services was established as part of a reorganization and extension of Alibaba's financial business, and the microloan business was renamed "Ant Micro Loan." This then merged with MYBank, continuing to serve self-employed and small-scale businesses with "online business loans." In 2016, it launched microfinance products for individuals, called Ant Credit Pay, and Ant Cash Now. This case study explores how Ant Micro Loan developed a credit model based on online transactions. It looks at the options they face in expanding their financing channels and funding sources. Moreover, it considers the social value of digital inclusive financing as represented by this small loan business.

Birth and development of the microloan business

The birth of the microloan business stemmed from the problems and benefits that emerged from the development of Alibaba's e-commerce

---

1   This case is based on the 2014 case of Professor Chen Long, Alibabas Micro Loans: Merchant Credit Cards, adapted and updated by Case Researcher Yang Yan.

platform. Companies which rely on the Alibaba platform are mainly small and micro-enterprises, long-tail clients for which traditional banks have difficulty providing cover. The problems these companies have in obtaining loans from banks limit their development and curtail the healthy growth of the Alibaba platform itself. But the large amount of enterprise data and credit information accumulated by the Alibaba platform laid the foundation for the development of its microloan business.

The "China TrustPass (CXT)" value-added service launched by the Alibaba B2B platform accumulated first-hand data from merchants, and in 2004, Alibaba launched a corporate rating system, "Integrity Index," based on the "Integrity Files" of its members. In 2006, Alibaba Group began testing the waters of the microloan business. Given its advantages in data resources but lack of experience in financial services, Alibaba first tried to work with the banks. For traditional financial institutions, such as banks, there are two main problems with the microloan business. First, there is generally a lack of transparency on the financial status of small and micro-enterprises, and with their limited capital size and lack of collateral assets, it is expensive and difficult for the banks to assess them. Second, it is particularly difficult to monitor the credit status of such small companies as a result of the slow development of China's credit system. There is a high degree of instability and moral hazard in the operation of small and micro-enterprises, which presents a challenge for banks in terms of such elements as post-lending management and risk control.

Alibaba offered a solution to these problems. At that time, there were 37 million small and micro-enterprises across the country doing business on the Alibaba platform, and the platform had information on them that had been accumulated over many years. Based on that data, Alibaba could help banks screen customers and control risk. In June 2007, Alibaba cooperated with China Construction Bank (CCB) and Industrial and Commercial Bank of China (ICBC) to launch a small business loan called "Ali Loan." For Ali Loan, small businesses did not need to provide any collateral, and any combination of three or more companies could form a consortium to apply for a loan.

However, in the initial phase, cooperation between Alibaba and the banks did not go well. Alibaba introduced about 27,000 B2B customers to CCB, but ultimately less than 10% of them secured loans. Hu Xiaoming, then the senior director of Alibaba's Credit Payment Department, said that, "three years of cooperation with banks has failed. Within the entire Chinese economic ecosystem, banks are supposed to serve large and medium-sized enterprises while financial services aimed at small and micro-enterprises should be handled through technological innovation."

While the effort to cooperate with banks was not successful, the experience helped Alibaba to establish a full range of credit evaluation systems and credit databases, as well as loan risk control mechanisms. On this foundation, Alibaba Group began to independently develop a "microloan business."

In March 2010, Zhejiang Alibaba Small Loan Company was established, the first domestic microfinance company specializing in lending to online merchants, and Chongqing Alibaba Small Loan Company was founded in 2011. Since then, the microloan business providing credit loans to small and micro-enterprises and individual sellers on the Ali e-commerce system has witnessed rapid growth. The first-year loan balance was about RMB 100 million, and rose to about RMB 12 billion in the third year.

With the formal establishment of Ant Financial Services in 2014, the microloan business was integrated into Ant Financial Group and re-named "Ant Micro Loan" with an expansion of its service target from small and micro-enterprises within the Ali platform to enterprises beyond the platform as well. As an online loan company, Ant Micro Loan actually operates a banking credit business, but also faces many restrictions, such as those related to sourcing funds and business scope. As a result, with more than five years of microloan operational experience, Ant Financial Services integrated its financial data and technical resources, and it began to develop into a private bank. In September 2014, it received a first batch of private banking licenses from the China Banking Regulatory Commission (CBRC) and in June 2015, MYBank was formally established. Not long after that, the Ant Micro Loan business was integrated and merged into it.

At the time of its establishment, MYBank proposed to stick with the "small deposit and small loan" model, mainly providing deposit products under RMB 200,000 and loan products under RMB five million, while expanding financial services originally provided to small and micro-enterprises to rural areas and also setting a target of serving ten million customers within five years. As of the end of 2016, the microloan business incorporated into MYBank had provided financing services to more than 2.77 million small and micro customers.

Microcredit business operation model

Information asymmetry is the core challenge in finance, which is especially true for small and micro financial services. One measure of the efficiency of financial services is how to identify risks at a lower cost. Compared with large and medium-sized enterprises, risk screening of small and micro-enterprises is difficult and costly, making it a business area that cannot be fully covered by commercial banks. Based on the long-tail effect of the Internet and the support of digital technology, digital finance as represented by Ant Micro Loan, uses rich data resources to establish corporate credit and risk control systems, to reduce at a small cost the information asymmetry associated with small and micro-enterprises. This becomes the core advantage and the key operational factor. But improving data and credit information is still the greatest difficulty encountered in the operation of the microloan business.

Building the microloan model: Complete data jigsaw puzzle

The core team members of Alibaba's microloan business in the early stages came mainly from the banking industry, mostly with experience in the credit markets. In establishing its own operating model, the team had a wealth of credit experience, and also had a theoretical base for reference, the FICO credit score model. But to truly provide credit independently, the microloan teams needed to overcome a huge challenge, namely a limited amount of data. Although the Ali platform had accumulated information on millions of small and micro-enterprises and individual sellers, this was just the "tip of the iceberg" in terms of international credit rating requirements for individuals. In the case of the U.S., which has the world's most-developed credit system, the content of credit ratings is all-embracing. In addition to the length of the period covered by traditional credit records, credit lines, overdue loans, mortgage records and other information, non-financial information on individuals such as criminal records are also included. For corporate information, some credit bureaus even include information such as the geographical distance between the registered address of the company and the area code of the contact telephone.

At that time, the microloan business was facing a relatively closed credit information environment. The People's Bank of China's Credit Information System, which includes basic corporate credit data and basic personal credit information, is a relatively complete information collection system, but it was then only open to commercial banks and other financial institutions. In addition, government departments such as public security, the courts, customs, industry and commerce and taxation as well as non-government organizations such as commercial banks, public utilities, postal services and telecommunications also had a large amount of corporate and personal credit information that conformed to international practices, but was scattered and silo-ed.

Third-party credit agencies in China are not yet mature, and the information available for reference is limited. At that time, the public departments and organizations of only a few regions, such as the industry and commerce departments, banks, telecommunications and public utilities, were open to third-party credit bureaus. In addition, if individual credit bureaus want to obtain comprehensive and reliable credit information, it requires cooperation from various departments which, in the absence of support from the relevant laws and regulations, is difficult to achieve.

Data was limited in nature and dispersed, leaving the microloan team with no option but to try every method to complete the credit information jigsaw puzzle, including requiring the lender to provide relevant information, purchasing third-party credit information and obtaining data from customs, taxation, electricity, water and other departments. In the microloan company's second year of operations, Alibaba was given access to the People's Bank of China's credit information system, greatly enriching the available data. Later, the microloan business also cooperated with the ERP enterprise management software GJP, which has SMEs as its customer base, and the national unified value-added tax invoice software Aisino, in order to acquire company production, inventory, sales and other data, opening up many other channels.

Next, the microloan business needed to integrate internal and external data, and build its own credit models and processes. There is a "data workshop" within the system which is responsible for aggregating and analyzing the data stored by merchants on the Taobao[2] and Tmall[3] platforms, including transaction growth and volatility, a star evaluation system for stores and traffic, advertising input and community behavior. This internal data, together with externally-sourced data, are packaged into hundreds of models developed by Alibaba, including customer stratification models,

---

2   Alibaba's online shopping platform.
3   Taobao's B2C channel.

revenue forecast models, bankruptcy probability models, and early warning risk models.

By this time, a quantitative, automatic loan approval model had been established. After a seller makes a loan application, all relevant data will be imported into the model, and the model will make a judgment on whether or not to make the loan. The original general manager of Alibaba Group's microloan business, Lou Jianxun, said that to resolve problems like forecasting the behavior curve of Taobao sellers required the construction of 192 data models. Compared with traditional credit, the richness of the model quantities and data input is a unique advantage of Ant Micro Loan.

Application of the microloan model: Product categories

In the early stages of the microloan business, the main loan products launched included Taobao (Tmall) credit loans, Taobao (Tmall) order loans and Ali credit loans. Taobao (Tmall) credit loans and order loans are for Ali platform sellers, while Ali credit loans provides B2B loans to Alibaba China site members and China suppliers.

Taobao (Tmall) loans

The quantitative loan issuance model was first applied in Taobao and Tmall. The microloan team believes that since the Taobao (Tmall) platform has more complete and reliable trading information and data, it is relatively easy to provide loans to sellers on this platform. In addition, many such sellers rely on the online business for their livelihood and as the cost of default is high, the risk of default is relatively low.

The so-called "order loan" refers to applications made by Taobao (Tmall) sellers based on their store's status that indicates the seller has already shipped the product, which is basically the same as an order-collateralized loan. For order loans and credit loans, merchants complete the loan application online, submit the relevant materials and enter the automatic approval process, the loan model will be automatically scored to determine whether the loan should be issued and how much should be lent. Since order loan products are generated based on actual transactions on the Taobao (Tmall) platform, a loan can be released to the merchant's Alipay account within three minutes.

By the end of 2012, the average single amount of a Taobao order loan was about RMB 4,900, and the average single Tmall order loan amount was around RMB 21,000. Microloans small in scale but large in quantity raise the requirements in terms of cost control, which is one of the reasons why traditional banks are unable to take on microfinance. But when the microloan business's basic platform and process has been put in place, the cost of a single credit operation is greatly reduced.

In the lending and post-lending phase, the microloan business can at any time monitor the company's transaction status and cash flow through the Taobao (Tmall) platform and the Alipay system. If a loan is actually used in production and operations, the client's platform traffic will increase and the turnover and profit will also rise. Conversely, if the evaluation results worsen, an early warning is given and early repayment of the loan will be required. Any behavior affecting normal performance, such as an interruption to an Ali Wangwang[4] login, the purchase of a large number of lottery tickets with sales revenue or concentrated advertising, will raise an alert. If a company is in breach of a contract, the microloan team can cut off the customer's cash flow through Alipay and at the same time implement an online shop closure mechanism.

Increasing the cost of customer default by such measures helps to control loan risk. It is very difficult for traditional credit institutions to keep track of the use of loan funds in the post-loan period, but on the Taobao platform, the seller's use of capital and operations can be partially monitored, which is a major advantage of Ant Micro Loan.

Ali Credit Loans (B2B)

However, when it comes to B2B customers, it is difficult to follow the same set of processes. Compared with the Taobao (Tmall) platform, the B2B platform accumulated very limited data, Alibaba's B2B website is similar to the "yellow pages," where buyers and sellers meet on the platform and then communicate privately. Information about whether a transaction takes place and for what amount and what the buyer's view is on this is not captured by the platform. At the same time, since the B2B website mainly provides a means of displaying capabilities, it is not "sticky" in terms of the merchants;

---

4   A real-time trading communication tool launched by Alibaba.

transactions between merchants do not require Alipay support, and there is no capital accumulation on Alipay that results. Therefore, the microloan business has lower post-loan control over the business, and the penalty for breach of contract is also relatively limited.

To solve the problem of limited information, the microloan team conducts online video surveys of potential customers, and also outsources due diligence work to local third-party agencies. Investigators from third-party agencies pay visits to companies and do interviews to help them create a simplified financial statement. These videos and data are uploaded to the back office, and the back office assesses the data by comparing it with corporate bank statements, credit system information, etc.

However, the microloan business does not have a good solution for controlling risk during and after the issuance of loans to B2B sellers. The funds do not stay in the Alipay system, which means the microloan business cannot monitor the effectiveness of the lender's use of funds, and can only strictly control repayment deadlines. If there is a breach of contract with a company, then a credit investigation is conducted. If it is determined that there is a problem with the company, then methods will be used to effect the return of the loan.

As Taobao (Tmall) loans serve an even larger group and have relatively mature and reliable technical support in the loan process and risk control, they account for 70% of the microloan products referred to above, while Ali credit loans (B2B) only account for about 30%. Of these, Taobao (Tmall) credit loans with no collateral and based on data alone made up the majority, accounting for 60% of all loans. On average, the non-performing and overdue rates for Ali credit loans are higher than for Taobao (Tmall) loans, which are also related to its relatively weak risk control system (see Table 1, Table 2).

Wang Nong Dai open up the rural market

After the microloan business was merged into MYBank, rural finance became one of the new directions for its business expansion. In November 2015, MYBank launched a microloan product called "Wang Nong Dai" for rural users, which mainly provides small-scale credit loans for animal breeders and micro-operators, extending the business of microloans into the rural market. As of the end of 2016, Wang Nong Dai had been implemented in 6,624 villages in 271 counties and cities in 25 provinces, with an average

Table 1: Comparison of Taobao (Tmall) Loans and Ali Credit Loans

	Tmall Credit	Tmall Order	Taobao Credit	Taobao Order	Ali Credit	Total
Loan balance (100 million RMB)	62.63	10.91	97.49	9.39	86.26	266.68
Loan balance proportion	23.49%	4.09%	36.56%	3.52%	32.35%	100.00%
Number of customers (10,000)	6.66	2.11	65.75	11.06	8.53	94.11
Proportion of number of customers	7.08%	2.24%	69.87%	11.75%	9.06%	100.00%
Default rate	2.08%	0.46%	2.50%	1.06%	2.56%	2.29%
Overdue rate	4.07%	0.64%	4.74%	1.60%	3.92%	4.04%

Source: Credit Rating Report of Ant Micro Loan Phase 7 Microloan Asset-backed Special Plan, up to June 2015

Table 2: Loan Ranges and Proportions

Scale of loans (RMB)	Tmall Credit (%)	Tmall Order (%)	Taobao Credit (%)	Taobao Order (%)	Ali Credit (%)
Less than 10,000	3.16	7.51	26.64	36.74	0.42
10,000-50,000	21.28	26.56	27.73	34.82	9.55
50,000-100,000	20.56	17.58	14.83	11.93	17.21
100,000-200,000	22.62	17.58	14.42	8.41	34.76
200,000-500,000	22.51	19.6	12.78	5.54	30.19
500,000-1000,000	8.67	7.14	3.34	2.24	6.86

Source: Credit Rating Report of Ant Loan Phase 7 Micro Loan Asset-backed Special Plan, up to June 2015

loan amount of nearly RMB 50,000.

The development of the rural microloan business faces much greater challenges than other types of microloan products. The backward nature of the rural financial infrastructure, imperfect or even non-existent information, and the limited nature of the collateral assets of rural households make the problems commonly found in microloans even more serious in rural areas. In this regard, Alibaba's "Rural Taobao" agenda became the vehicle for Ant Rural Financial Services.

Rural Taobao went online in October 2014 with an e-commerce platform mainly focused on cooperation with local governments to establish village-level service centers and develop the rural e-commerce market. As of the end of 2015, the number of such service centers exceeded 10,000, and had accumulated a wealth of data and information resources. The Rural Taobao partners play a crucial role in the process of issuing microloans in rural areas. After a screening process, partners can become Wang Nong Dai sponsors. Villagers submit loan applications online via the sponsor, complete their personal information, and provide proof of assets such as land, houses, shops etc. After a review by MYBank, the loan contract can be signed online and the loan process can be completed within an average of 3-5 days.

The role of the sponsor in each loan transaction is critical. In addition to assessing the borrower's credit status and repayment ability before the issuance of the loan, the sponsor is also responsible for post-loan management and reminding the farmers to make repayments in a timely fashion. For each loan, the sponsor can get a certain percentage of the commission, but the commission payment will be adjusted based on the follow-up behavior of the sponsor and online data, such as the loan default status. Underperforming sponsors will likely be eliminated, or in serious cases, may even face legal risks. This punishment mechanism for sponsors is also part of the loan risk control process.

The selection process of Rural Taobao partners involves various steps including a review of business and ethical standards, as well as professional training. The requirements for the sponsors of Wang Nong Dai are more stringent, and after further screening within the scope of the partners, only 10% of partners can become sponsors with responsibility for management of the loan business. Evaluations of the sponsor focus on the individual's

Table 3: Main Products of the Microloan Business

	Tmall/Taobao Loan		Ali Credit Loan	Wang Nong Dai
	Order Loan	Credit Loan		
Target	Taobao and Tmall seller	Taobao and Tmall seller	Members of Alibaba B2B Chinese site and Chinese suppliers	Rural small and micro operators covered by Rural Taobao
Product Introduction	Based on the order amount of the physical transaction that the seller's store has issued but the buyer has not confirmed, the overall store operations are evaluated, and the loan for the credit line is provided	Credit is granted on the basis of store management status and is not limited by the number of orders per day. No need for collateral guarantees, it can be used repeatedly within the credit limit, with loans made and returned at any time.	Rotating credit: get a certain amount as a reserve fund, no interest if not used, loans and repayment at any time. Fixed credit: the credit amount granted issued in one go	Partners of Rural Taobao serve as sponsors, collect information in Rural Taobao sites, provide unsecured and pure credit loans to farmers.
Credit line	Up to 1,000,000	Up to 1,000,000	Up to 500,000	Up to 500,000
Loan term	30 days	6/12 months	1 year	3/6/12/24 months
Interest rates and fees	Daily interest rate of about 0.05%, and specific data depending on credit and business status	Daily interest rate of about 0.05%, specific data different depending on time of the loan, credit of the borrower and operating conditions	Daily interest rate about 0.05%, lowest 0.038%, specific data depends on credit and business status	Annual interest rates of agricultural loans and commercial loans at 12% and 6.5% respectively. Specific data depend on regional, industrial and personal conditions
Repayment methods	System automatic repayment	Monthly interest payments, repayment of entire principal when due; monthly payment of fixed interest and principal	Binding with Alipay account, monthly repayment of principal and interest via Alipay after loan issuance	Monthly interest repayments, one-time repayment or equivalent principal repayment

Source: CKGSB Case Center

credit rating, including the Sesame Credit score[5], whether there are any irregularities in their Taobao platform operations, and even their record of cooperation with local governments. In a rural society where typically everyone knows everyone else, highly intensive communication with villagers is the main way to obtain personal credit, capabilities and other information. Through the collection and review of information about the farmers via the sponsors who are familiar with the villagers, combined with online data from the e-commerce platform providing a view on credit levels throughout the entire region, a risk control system integrating both offline and online can be created.

Sustainability: Sources of funds and financing channels

Initially, as a business operating under an ordinary small loan company, the loan amounts issued by Ant Micro Loan were limited by the leverage ratio set by the central bank and the China Banking Regulatory Commission (CBRC). According to the regulations, the capital taken in by a small loan company from banking financial institutions shall not exceed 50% of its net capital. In other words, Ant Micro Loan with registered capital of RMB 1.6 billion could only expand to RMB 2.4 billion using a leverage factor of 0.5. Only with continuous return of capital and continuous turnover could the accumulated loan quota be increased.

In order to solve the problem of sourcing capital and to expand the scale of the business, as early as 2012, Ali Small Loan (the predecessor of Ant Micro Loan) issued a trust plan through Shandong Trust, which raised RMB 360 million in funds. But due to the private nature of the trust plan, the financing scale was limited and the cost of financing was relatively high.

Since 2013, Ant Micro Loan has been trying to raise funds using a relatively more efficient approach – asset securitization. In July 2013, Chongqing Alibaba Small Loan Company, the main issuer, cooperated with Orient Securities on a plan to launch ten separate issues, each with RMB200-500 million of asset-backed securities maturing in 1-2 years. This was the first domestic asset securitization product for securities companies based

---

5 Also known as Zhima Credit. A private credit scoring system and loyalty program developed by Ant Financial. It uses data from Alibaba's services to compile its score. Customers receive a score based on a variety of factors related to social media interactions and purchases carried out on Alibaba websites or paid for using Alipay.

on microloans, and was listed on the Shenzhen Stock Exchange. After its integration with Ant Financial Services in 2015, Chongqing Alibaba Small Loan Company and CICC (China International Capital Corporation) launched another special plan for microloan securitization, with a scale of RMB 5.5 billion.

Since the period for each loan in the microloan business is relatively short while the term of the securitized product is relatively long, the maturity mismatch is addressed by using rollover issuance of financing – that is, repaid funds are used to purchase new loans until the securities mature.

In addition, in order to improve the rating of microloan securitization products, internal credit enhancement and external credit enhancement have been adopted in the securitization process. Internal credit is divided into senior, mezzanine and junior tranches according to different risk and return characteristics. With Orient Securities/Alibaba's first securitized issue, the three types of rating securities accounted for 75%, 15% and 10% respectively. The issue's senior tranche was sold to ordinary investors while the junior tranche was purchased by Alibaba; in CICC-Ant Financial's issue, the proportion of senior tranche rose to 78%, and the mezzanine tranche fell to 12%. In terms of external credit enhancement, Shangcheng Financial

Table 4: Ant Micro Loan Securitization Products

Financing body	Financing method	Financing period	Use of funds	Scale	Cost of funds
Chongqing Alibaba Small Loan Co., Ltd.	Orient Securities-Ali ABS	2013-2014	Micro loan for company operation	5 billion RMB	Average 7.8%
	CICC Micro Loan ABS	2015	Micro loan for company operations	5.5 billion RMB	Average 6.3%
	Deppon-Ant Cash Now ABS	2016-2018	Personal consumer loans	79.6 billion RMB	Average 5.1%
Chongqing Ali Micro Loan Co. Ltd.	Deppon-Ant Credit Pay ABS	2016-2018	personal consumer loan	102.6 billion RMB	Average 4.9%

Source: Wind, CKGSB Case Center

Guarantee Company, owned by Ant Financial Services, provides guarantee services within the scope of the warranty at the expiry of the term. With internal and external credit enhancement, Ant Micro Loan's senior tranche of asset-backed securities received an AAA rating.

After MYBank's establishment in 2015, it became the main source of funds for microloans, while the asset securitization products issued by small loan companies were mainly used for personal credit products such as "Ant Credit Pay" and "Ant Cash Now" (see Table 4).

However, as it has not yet obtained permission for remote account opening, MYBank is so far unable to absorb deposits on a large scale, and the lending of funds to small and micro customers is therefore limited. It mainly relies upon inter-bank lending and non-bank deposits of fund companies and insurance companies, and compared to traditional banks, capital costs are high. Therefore, expanding the channels of funding has become even more important. Yu Shengfa, the former president of MYBank, stated that "asset securitization is a very important channel for MYBank's future

Table 5: Comparison of the Average Expected Yield of Senior Tranches of ABS Products and the SHIBOR Spread

Issuer	Product	Yield	Interest rate of SHIBOR in the same period	Spread
Large Internet micro loan platform	Ant Cash Now	5.10%	3%	2.10%
	Ant Credit Pay	4.90%	3%	1.90%
	JD IOUs	5.50%	3%	2.50%
	Xiaomi Small Loan	6%	3%	3%
Emerging Internet micro loan platforms	Yirendai	6.50%	3%	3.50%
	Fenqile	6.00%	3.20%	2.80%
	China Top Credit	5.80%	3%	2.80%
Commercial banks	Ping An Bank	3.50%	3.20%	0.30%
	Bank of Nanjing	3.25%	3.05%	0.20%
	China Merchants Bank	3.30%	3%	0.30%

Source: 01Caijing, by CKGSB Case Center

funding sources, and as asset securitization becomes more and more mature and the level of market acceptance rises, our ability to raise funds in the market will also be strengthened. This will play a very important supportive role in the development of MYBank." It is understood that MYBank's first asset securitization product was launched at the end of 2016. Compared with previous small loan companies, the capital costs of the asset securitization products issued by MYBank, as a "commercial bank," should be relatively low (see Table 5).

The social value of Ant Micro Loan

At the 2016 G20 summit in Hangzhou, inclusive finance was one of the important topics. Unlike traditional financial services that mainly serve "top" users, inclusive finance aims to offer services to all social groups and individuals, so that equality and prosperity for the entire society can be realized. The realization of this goal is inseparable from the technical driving force, namely digital inclusive finance.

We know that finance is different from general "standardized" commodities, and for both traditional finance and digital finance, information asymmetry is the biggest challenge. Financial institutions traditionally provided individualized financial services for all, meaning they had to shoulder the whole burden of cost pressures resulting from individual information asymmetry. Today, digital finance is driven by technology and allows institutions for the first time in history to know customers and identify risks using remote means which, combined with the traditional process of financial services, significantly reduces costs.

The genes that Ant Micro Loan has inherited are matched with the core elements of inclusive finance. In the context of digital inclusive – i.e. "universal benefits" – finance, Ant Micro Loan has expanded financial services channels through the Internet platform, achieving "universal" in terms of service coverage, and has reduced the cost of micro-credit loans through big data and financial cloud technologies, thereby also achieving benefits. In addition, Ant Financial Services' all-round development of financial services, such as payments, financing, wealth management, insurance and credit, as well as the sustainability of its business models, coincide with the comprehensiveness and sustainability of inclusive finance.

However, to achieve fully-fledged, full-coverage "inclusive finance," the platform needs to have more comprehensive information and create richer and more diversified scenario resources, which might be limited by existing platform ecosystems. To a certain extent, the degree of integration with commercial scenarios will become an important criterion for future financial development. At present, the main targets of the micro-credit loan service are still the small and micro enterprises on the Ali platform. Therefore, the expansion of the platform ecosystem and the innovation of scenarios are important breakthrough points for the future of micro loans and even of Ant Financial Services. The degree of integration with business scenarios will to a certain extent become an important criterion for future financial development.

As an ecosystem platform for Ant Micro Loan, Ant Financial Services is accelerating the pace of "scenario-based" financial strategies. Peng Lei, former CEO of Ant Financial Services Group, has said on several occasions that the future of Internet finance is scenario-based. Financial services, including payments, wealth management, financing, insurance, and so on, are closely linked to everyone's daily lives. Therefore, the development direction of "scenario-based finance" is in a way consistent with the characteristics and concepts of inclusive finance.

Take Alipay for example. Since its 9.0 release in July 2015, it has evolved from a "payment platform" into a "scenario platform." Fan Zhiming, president of the Payment Group of Ant Financial Services, said: "In the past, people were busy chasing various scenarios, and life became more and more fragmented. But the new Alipay wants to place people at the center, allowing consumer, financial management, life, communication and other scenarios to be re-configured in a human-centric way to allow, through big data and Internet technology, for services to become more personalized and friendlier."

Ant Micro Loan – created to solve the problem of financing for small and micro enterprises on the Taobao e-commerce platform – and "Wang Nong Dai," created to solve the problem of farmer loans – together with the individual consumer credit business, are products that address concrete funding issues. In recent years, MYBank has also made many attempts at scenario innovation. For example, it cooperates with the CNZZ platform, the world's largest Chinese language website traffic statistics operator, to extend the reach of the Ant Financial Services platform to launch "word-of-mouth loans" for offline F&B catering businesses, and a variety of higher-value financial credit products for such specific scenarios as promotion loans for "Double 11" mass shopping day. Some of the innovations break away from the Ali system and use technological advantages to collaborate with other platforms to provide loans to small and micro enterprises outside the Ali platform, and also use the ecosystems of new platforms to provide credit services to offline small and micro businesses. "Scenario loans" will also become the focus of future explorations and innovations by MYBank.

The "platformization" strategy that has been emphasized throughout has provided broader opportunities for Ant Financial to expand its platform and create new scenarios. On August 10, 2015, at its partner conference in Beijing, Ant Financial presented its fully-upgraded open platform, providing them with a wide range of capabilities on payments, credit, finance and technology, as well as information on huge numbers of small and micro merchants. Ant Financial is also able to use partner platform ecosystems and various scenarios to create and provide more financial services. For example, in June 2015, Ant Financial Services signed a strategic cooperation agreement with Industrial Bank to share resources in channels, businesses, products, customers, etc., and to cooperate in areas including rural finance, inclusive finance, and people's livelihood finance.

Today, China's economy has entered a "new normal" phase and the investment-led economic growth of the past is no longer sustainable. In the future, the driving forces for economic development will include personalized and diversified consumption, and smart and professional production. In this process of transformation, the entire financial system needs to shift towards consumer, mass and inclusive finance to meet the requirements of economic growth. Yi Gang, the governor of the People's Bank of China, has repeatedly stressed the importance of inclusive finance in the future direction of China's financial development, and Ant Micro Loan, as a pioneer in digital inclusive finance, is closely linked to the future development of China's economy and society, creating a social value that goes far beyond commercial value.

10. Qihoo 360

The Road Back to China

Supervising Supervisor: Li Wei; Case Researchers: Yang Yan, Liu Xiaoting

Internet security company Qihoo 360 was listed on the New York Stock Exchange in 2011, and strong earnings performance led its share price to rise steadily thereafter. At one point, shares topped US$100, making Qihoo 360 the third-largest Chinese internet company by market capitalization. Meanwhile, shifts in the company's internal structure and changes in the external environment – particularly the steady relaxation of China's capital markets policies and an A-share[1] bull market – forced founder Zhou Hongyi to review Qihoo's strategy.

Joining a wave of privatization among overseas-listed Chinese concept stocks (CCS)[2] in 2015, Qihoo 360's journey back to the Chinese A-share market gained considerable attention for its scale and high valuation.

Going Public in America

Qihoo 360 went public on March 30, 2011 when it was only in its fifth year of operation. Founder Zhou Hongyi had taken his Qihoo 360 team on a sweep of the Internet with their free security software – 360 Safeguard[3]. Eager

---

1 A-share are shares denominated in RMB and traded on the Shanghai and Shenzhen stock exchanges, as well as National Equities Exchange and Quotations (NEEQ), China's over-the-counter corporate share trading market.

2 China Concept Stocks are companies which have a significant proportion of their assets or earnings in mainland China but which are listed overseas to gain access to foreign investor capital. There are China Concepts Stocks listed on several major stock exchanges around the globe, including HKEx, NASDAQ, NYSE etc.

3 360 Safeguard's focus is on stopping malware such as computer viruses and trojan horses, and providing security patches for Microsoft Windows.

downloaders were then offered other software, including a desktop software manager and a potent Antivirus package, while Qihoo 360 continued to up its Internet security user numbers. The company proceeded to enter the browser, site map and software download sectors, accumulating a vast user base.

In its IPO prospectus, Qihoo 360 described itself as third among Chinese internet companies in user base size and second in terms of number of connected terminals, and the second-largest browser company in China after Microsoft. Qihoo 360 said it was China's top Internet security solutions provider, with over 339 million users and a 85% penetration rate.

Foreign investors were skeptical of Qihoo 360's business model. It was an anti-virus software provider but most of its revenues came from advertisements. Its reported profit was only five U.S. cents per share, which meant the onus was on the company to prove it had significant profit potential. A commercial dispute with Tencent in the second half of 2010 also cast a shadow over Qihoo's reputation and performance.

But Zhou was pitching a story that Wall Street liked to hear – on his road shows, he called Qihoo 360 the "Chinese Facebook". He explained to investors how the company "did Internet security first to meet users' requirements on information security, and then used its browser to build an online platform and provide value-added services through the desktop manager service." The outcome was a listing success beyond his expectations. Foreign investors, he declared, understood its business model and saw it as "an extremely innovative company."

Qihoo 360 successfully issued U.S. depository receipts for 12.1 million shares and raised US$175 million in an IPO that was 40 times over-subscribed. On the first day of trading, Qihoo shares closed at US$34, an increase of 134.5% over its listing price of US$14.50, becoming the latest "miracle of Wall Street". Its market capitalization reached US$3.956 billion, ranking it sixth among all CCS companies. The equity structure following the IPO left Zhou Hongyi, Chairman of the Board and CEO, with 18.46% of the shares, while another founder and President of Qihoo, Qi Xiangdong, held 10.67%.

In the face of such a stock price surge on the first day of trading, Zhou Hongyi was quite composed. The share price was not his concern, he said, and going public was just a start. There was still a lot of hard work to be done over the following five to ten years. "The market decides the stock price for Qihoo 360," he said. "Qihoo 360 accepts whatever the market decides." He added that the most important thing about going public for Qihoo was not raising capital, but proving "the desire to improve the brand and attract more talent."

A partner with CDH Investments[4], shared in the IPO excitement and wrote on social media, "Based to the stock price today, our investment has earned US$200 million", amounting to a 40 times return on a five-year investment. In March, 2006, Qihoo had held its A round of financing, taking in US$20 million from investors including Zhou Hongyi, Sequoia Capital, IDG and CDH. The B round of US$25 million was completed in November 2006, with Highland Capital leading and Redpoint Ventures participating, and investors from the A round, including Sequoia, CDH, Matrix and IDG also joining in.

Market commentators attributed the success of Qihoo 360's public listing to three major factors. First was the overall investment environment. The global economy was on a downward trend, while the Chinese Internet-based company model was seen by investors as very promising. Their success on NYSE and NASDAQ appeared to confirm their growth potential. Second, the innovative nature of the industry raised expectations for investors about future performance and profitability. The third factor was Qihoo 360's five consecutive years of profit, its unique model and its huge user base.

Embracing a Turn

Zhou Hongyi was surprised that during the years following the IPO, Qihoo 360 continued to attract a huge amount of attention. With its stabilized user base, growing advertising revenues and profitable value-added services, the company maintained close to 100% annual revenue growth from 2011 to 2013, the stock price continued to rise and at one point even exceeded US$100, making Qihoo 360 China's third largest internet company by market capital.

Even when Chinese concept stocks encountered a shorting crisis which led many of them to privatize, Zhou Hongyi remained true to his stock market decision. After the company was attacked by short-seller Citron Research six times, Zhou maintained that, "Listed companies are relatively transparent, and while enjoying the significant benefits of foreign capital

---

4   It is a major Chinese alternative asset management firm based in Beijing, China. It specializes in private equity, venture capital and credit products

markets and investors, we must also accept the assessment of the markets and should also accept true volatility in market valuation," he said. "Qihoo 360 will stick to its path (of being a public company in the U.S.)"[5]

The turning point came in 2014, when the release of the 2014 Q1 financial report indicated the company was trapped in a vicious performance and price cycle. The company had been issuing fantastic quarterly reports yet the stock price, after experiencing a short peak, had trended downwards (See Figure 1). By the end of May 2015, Qihoo's market value had shrunk to US$6.4 billion, less than half of its highest level.

Zhou Hongyi was forced to review the drastic changes taking place both within and outside Qihoo 360.

Figure 1: Stock Price Status of Qihoo 360 after going public

Source: CKGSB Case Center

Business Transformation

With the growth of mobile Internet, Baidu, Alibaba, Tencent and Xiaomi were all expanding their business operations and establishing ecosystems, and their stock prices were rising. Qihoo 360 felt left behind, its share price was falling steadily and its position was increasingly shaky.

---

5   "With Market Value Half its Peak, Qihoo 360 Might Turn to Privatization," Yicai.com, 2015.6.17, see http://www.yicai.com/news/4633655.html

While its traditional business operations were generating profits, PC traffic had been flat to declining in recent years. Also under threat by competitors in the mobile area, the company found it hard to gain support in the capital markets. Data showed that monthly user growth for Qihoo 360 products and services based on PCs was slowing while competitors such as Cheetah Mobile, Baidu, Tencent, Sogou, etc., were increasingly active in mobile security and search.

Faced with internal and external pressures, Qihoo 360 embarked on a business transformation.

First up was corporate security. In September 2013, Qihoo 360 released three new security products – 360 Skylar, Sky Eye and Tianji, targeting government and enterprise markets. When compared to the RMB 2 billion personal security market, the RMB 20 billion enterprise-level security market provided the company with greater development potential. But the personal and corporate markets were completely different, and the free strategy Qihoo 360 had used in the personal sphere could not be directly applied to business users.

Second was smart hardware. Over the previous year, Qihoo 360 had announced a strategic cooperation with Coolpad[6] and introduced two phone brands, Qiku and Dazen. It had also promoted smart hardware products including smart watches for kids, routers, smart cameras and driving recorder software TripREC. However, despite Zhou's great expectations, the market did not catch on – Qihoo 360 was a late-comer and did not have an advantageous position.

Third was Internet services. In order to find new growth points, Qihoo 360 followed Baidu, Alibaba and Tencent into gaming, films & television, medical care, media and other fields, and introduced corresponding Internet services.

Zhou hoped that in the era of the "Internet-of-Everything," Qihoo 360 could develop as a company combining hardware, software and the Internet – the core applications, underscored by the key word "security".

Different Valuations in China and America

During the second half of 2014, a great disparity opened up between the

---

6   A Chinese telecommunications equipment company headquartered in Shenzhen, Guangdong

Figure 2: Valuations in the Chinese and U.S. Markets, end-May 2015

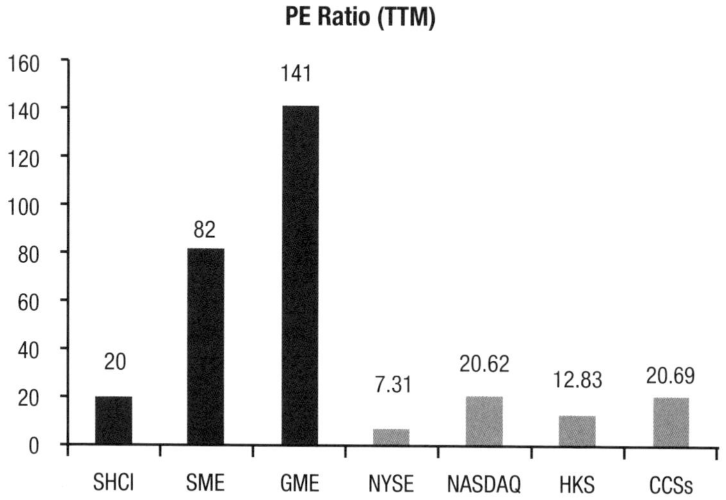

PE Ratio (TTM)

Source: Wind

A-share market and the U.S. stock markets. By the end of May 2015, the three major stock indices of China's stock market – SHCI[7], SME[8] and GEM[9] were up by 125%, 150% and 176% respectively from January 1, but the NASDAQ index was up only 13.7%, and the HXC index[10] representing CCS companies was also up only 8.3%, well behind the performance of the A-share market's indices. Valuations on the two markets also saw a great divergence. The average Price to Earnings (PE) ratios on the SHCI, SME and GEM were 20, 82 and 141 respectively, while NYSE and NASDAQ were only 7 and 21, and the average PE ratio for the CCS stocks in the U.S. was only 21.

Such a disparity was also seen in individual stocks. As the leader in China's cyber security industry, Qihoo 360 delivered excellent results in both 2014 and 2015, yet its PE ratio was stuck between 30 and 40. Meanwhile

---

7   Shanghai Stock Exchange Composite Index tracks the daily price performance of all companies listed on the Shanghai Stock Exchange.

8   The benchmark and flagship index of the SME (Small and Medium-sized Enterprises) Board of the Shenzhen Stock Exchange.

9   The benchmark and flagship Index of the GEM (Growth Enterprise Market) Board of the Shenzhen Stock Exchange.

10 Abbreviation of the Halter USX China Index.

Figure 3: A-share Market and U.S. Market Performance 2014-2015

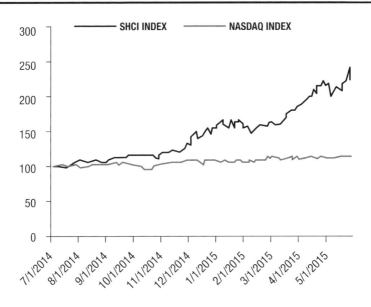

Note: 2014/7/1 = 100. Data as of 2015/5/31

Source: Wind, Bloomberg

in the A-share market, another major information security operator, Venus Tech, saw its share price rise from RMB 20 to RMB 73.1 in just a few months, with a PE ratio of 200. What was more, the valuation of Qihoo 360 fell way behind the other Internet companies on the GEM board. By the end of May 2015, LeTV had a PE ratio of 335, and Baofeng Tech[11] set a new record with a PE ratio of 900.

In fact, the lower valuations in the U.S. compared to the A-share market was an issue not just for Qihoo 360, but for many CCSs in a variety of industries. According to statistics from Analysys, by the end of the fourth quarter in 2014, China Mobile Games & Entertainment Group (CMGE) ranked top in the domestic mobile game market with a 20.1% market share, while Kunlun Game ranked fourth with a share of 10.3%. But Kunlun, listed in China, was valued at RMB 43.7 billion (US$6.7 billion), and CMGE, listed overseas, had a valuation of only US$620 million.[12] As Chen Tianqiao, CEO

11 LeTV and Baofeng Tech are both Internet video providers.
12 Data by the end of May, 2015.

of Shanda Interactive Entertainment[13], stated frankly, "Wall Street doesn't understand Chinese gaming."

Another example was the film and television industry. As one of the top five private film/TV companies in China, Bona Film achieved a valuation in the United States of US$777 million (around RMB 5 billion), while Huayi Brothers and Enlight Media in the same industry received valuations in the A-share market of RMB 52.4 billion (US$7.63 billion) and RMB 47.8 billion (US$6.96 billion) respectively.[14]

Zhou believed that in the same way, Qihoo 360 was being undervalued in the U.S. compared to A-share Internet companies such as Baofeng Tech and LeTV, in two ways. There was a major disparity in stock valuations between the Chinese and U.S. capital markets. On top of this, the U.S. capital market did not understand the Chinese Internet sector, especially operators with business models like Qihoo 360 which provide free software while profiting from other channels such as ad sales.

Capital Market Changes

There have been several waves of Chinese Internet companies listing overseas, especially in the US. A generally accepted explanation of this well-noted phenomenon is historical factors. In the 1990s, China's capital markets were dominated by an approval system that set rigid listing thresholds and standards, leaving basically unprofitable Internet companies with little chance of gaining eligibility. But in the United States, the threshold was low with no profitability requirement. Also, the capital market system there was mature and the listing process fast and welcoming of Chinese Internet companies. NYSE and NASDAQ provided relatively good support for high-tech companies and were able to offer high valuations. For many years, listing on the U.S. capital markets was a chief target of Chinese Internet company founders. In addition, many Chinese Internet companies had also had international investors from the start so their management structures had often laid the foundation for a future overseas listing.

But the shorting crisis beginning in 2010 changed the situation for CCS companies in the U.S. Short-selling operators including Citron Research and Muddy Waters Research hunted down CCS firms, targeting financial frauds,

---

13 A Chinese operator of online games and book publisher.
14 Data as of end-May, 2015

with New Oriental, Orient Paper[15], Rino International[16] attacked among others. Subsequently, the VIE (Variable Interest Entity)[17] incident triggered by Alipay[18] raised concerns about the structure with U.S. investors, which prompted short-sellers to launch a second round of attacks. Many CCS companies experienced a large fall in market value, leading to the withdrawal from the U.S. markets of Shanda, Focus Media[19] and many others. That was the beginning of the privatization and re-listing trend.

Meanwhile, the Chinese capital markets were developing gradually, with the creation of a multi-layered capital market system and better institutions, especially with regard to emerging industries. The changes created the conditions for CCS to re-list in China. With its relatively low threshold and its transfer mechanism[20], the newly-launched OTC system[21] attracted a large number of companies. At the same time, the Shanghai and Shenzhen stock exchanges respectively established a strategic board for emerging industries and relaxed conditions on the GEM board to support A-share listings by not-yet-profitable Internet companies. The circumstances of the strategic boards were particularly favorable, as Liu Shi'an, former Vice-President of the Shanghai Stock Exchange, noted: "The lower threshold on the strategic boards for emerging industries opens the way for overseas-listed Chinese

---

15 A paper-making company which was accused by the investigative investment firm Muddy Waters Research of financial fraud, including exaggerating income and misappropriating funds.

16 A manufacturing enterprise producing energy-saving and environmental protection equipment, accused by Muddy Waters Research of financial fraud, including exaggerating income, false contracts and customers, and misappropriating funds.

17 The VIE structure was devised to allow Chinese companies in industries with heavy restrictions on foreign ownership, typically sensitive telecommunications and technology, to list on overseas exchanges. The structure involves a China-based entity that holds the necessary permits and licenses to operate in China, and an overseas-based entity listed offshore. The offshore listed company typically has a wholly-owned subsidiary Chinese "shell" company, which enters into contractual agreements with the Chinese entity. Contracts between the two stipulate that the Chinese company transfers its profits to the shell company as its primary beneficiary in the form of fees and royalties. The Chinese entity is the VIE, in the sense that variable interest is created through contractual agreements by allowing offshore shareholders the appearance of control of the Chinese entity. The contracts do not guarantee the interests of foreign shareholders, as the offshore company does not own an equity stake in or have direct access to assets of the Chinese entity, which conducts the "real" businesses.

18 Alibaba transferred assets from Alipay, its online payment system, to a private company under Jack Ma's name, to the futile protests of major shareholders such as Yahoo Inc.

19 A Chinese company which operates the largest out-of-home advertising network in that country, consisting predominantly of digital signage screens, and claims to own the country's largest Internet advertising agency.

20 Companies listed on the OTC system can be upgraded to the main board when they meet certain conditions.

21 A Chinese over-the-counter system for trading the shares of a public limited company that is not listed on either the Shenzhen or Shanghai stock exchanges, also known as the NEEQ (National Equities Exchange and Quotations) exchange.

companies, and provides systemic support for markets to accept CCSs." The expected implementation of a registration system for stock listings was also a major factor. Xiao Gang, former Chairman of the China Securities Regulatory Commission (CSRC), said in 2015 that conditions for the registration system were already in place, ready to be launched as soon as the new Securities Law went into effect.

Policy positions on the VIE issue regarding the return of CCSs were also being constantly relaxed, making the process more convenient. In April 2015, a revised draft of the Securities Law was issued containing four clauses relating to the domestic listing of Chinese companies currently listed elsewhere. In early June, during a State Council standing committee session, Premier Li Keqiang expressed clear support for the domestic listing of startup companies with special stock-ownership structures. Various ministries and commissions were also considering revisions to existing policies and the Ministry of Industry and Information was planning a relaxation of restrictions on foreign stock-ownership proportions, clearing the way for VIE-model companies to move to the A-share market. Both the Shanghai Stock Exchange and the Shenzhen Stock Exchange were studying plans for accepting companies with special stock-ownership structures.

Choosing Privatization

During the first half of 2015, A-share stocks were generally moving upwards, and investors were crazy for "concept" stocks. As the first Internet company to remove its VIE structure for a return to the A-share market, Baofeng Tech had over 30 limit-up trading days in March and April of that year, inspiring many companies with VIE structures to follow suit, and initiating the second wave of CCS returns.

It was in such a context that Zhou Hongyi considered the privatization of Qihoo 360.

CCS firms need to take three steps to effect a return, namely "privatization and delisting – removal of the VIE structure – reboot for listing".

Step 1. Privatization and delisting. Currently, the model used is mainly "Tender Offer plus Simple Merger", meaning that major shareholders make an offer to buy more than 90% of controlling shares, and then effect a simple merger. The whole process of privatization is complex and time-consuming, generally taking 6-12 months.

Step 2. Removal of the VIE structure. Many U.S.-listed CCS companies, especially those in the Internet and education fields, faced obstacles in terms of the "Catalogue Guiding Foreign Investments in Industry", a negative list for foreign investment access, and such companies would normally be required to remove the VIE structure, turn a foreign-invested enterprise into a Chinese domestic company, and then buy back the shares held by foreign investors. This process is complicated, involving the interests of various major parties, and hence time-consuming.

Step 3. Reboot for listing. At the time, there were three models for the move of CSS firms to the A-share market:

1. Direct application for IPO – Baofeng Tech was the first Internet company to return to the A-share market by removing its VIE structure and going IPO.
2. Backdoor listing – Many companies used this approach, including Focus Media which listed through Hedy.
3. The NEEQ Exchange. For companies not qualified for an A-share IPO, the OTC market has a lower threshold and a shorter process, allowing companies to first go public and then seek opportunities on other boards.

One of the widely recognized advantages of privatization is that companies can restructure in the process. For example, Alibaba B2B's retreat from HKEX triggered reorganization in preparation for a listing in the United States. For low-valuation and financing-challenged companies, delisting also reduces operational costs (including legal costs, compliance and finance costs). Furthermore, a re-listing on the A-share market also meant that valuations could be effectively improved, leading to more financing and more growth.

However, Zhou Hongyi also realized there are many difficulties involved in achieving a re-listing.

First, delisting is an extremely complex process including fixing a price for privatization, avoiding lawsuits and disputes with investors, and adjusting the equity structure without creating obstacles for a China listing.

Second, unwinding the VIE structure was not simply a matter of ending an agreement, as it required a re-allocation of assets into an entity that could go public domestically. There was a huge amount of work to be done in dealing with the commerce, tax and foreign affairs departments.

Another tricky issue involved U.S. funds which had been early investors; some wanted to follow the company back, and some did not. And for those that wanted to participate in a China re-listing, there was still the problem of how to fix the pricing of the transaction between U.S. funds and RMB funds. A myriad of complex relationships needed to be resolved.

Third, the unwinding of the VIE structure could lead, for smaller companies, to a new problem: Which board to choose for a re-listing, the NEEQ Exchange or the Strategic Emerging Industries Board?

It was precisely the complexity of all these steps that made the re-listing process so risky. The first problem was timing. A retreat from the U.S. market could take as long as 6-12 months with a considerable uncertainty remaining about the time required for re-listing on the domestic capital markets. At that time, in 2015, waiting in line for IPO approval could take two years or more. Also, there was still no clarity on the timing for the unveiling and implementation of an IPO registration system in place of the approval process. Of course, companies could choose to go directly to the NEEQ Exchange for a public listing, which reduced the waiting time. But its capital-raising capacity and liquidity were challenges. Another option would be a backdoor listing, but the cost of buying a shell for a listing was at least RMB 3 billion – Focus Media spent RMB 4 billion on acquiring one.

Another risk associated with a long delay was the possibility of missing the window of opportunity in the A-share market. In 2015, many CCS firms initiated the privatization process largely because the A-share surge opened up an arbitrage opportunity in cross-border valuations. A long delay could throw into question Qihoo 360's ability to catch the bull market wave. Also, the company needed to consider the sentiment of its staff who had been waiting a long lime for a chance to cash out their options. Would staff be willing to continue on this "Long March" with the company as it relocated to the China market?

Apart from the long delay between de-listing and re-listing, another risk to consider was financing costs. According to SEC requirements, shareholders choosing privatization must buy all tradable shares with cash. As buyers have to provide small and medium shareholders with a premium to the average stock price over a recent period, the financial pressure on buyers to reach the goal could skyrocket. CCS companies choosing privatization generally rely in outside financing or apply for bank loans. But delays can lead to leverage and cost problems that magnify the risks of privatization. Furthermore, companies still have to continue to do business during the de-listing / re-listing process, and must take care in handling financing issues during that period. Most companies incur large debts during the process, which also inhibits their financing capabilities.

Completing Privatization

After thorough discussions with some senior executives and major shareholders on the prospects of privatization and the challenges Qihoo 360 could encounter, Zhou Hongyi made the decision to go with privatization, and set the process in motion.

On June 17, 2015, Qihoo 360 announced it had accepted an initial non-binding offer from Zhou and other senior managers for privatization.

In December 2015, Qihoo 360 reached agreement with buyers led by Zhou and some other institutions[22] to purchase outstanding common stock of Qihoo at a price of USA$77 / ADS, in cash. The privatization transaction was valued at nearly US$9.3 billion.

In January 2016, China Merchants Bank led two other commercial banks in providing Qihoo 360 with debt financing of US$3.4 billion to facilitate the privatization, the largest leveraged buyout ever for a CCS firm.

On March 30, Qihoo 360 held an extraordinary general meeting and the privatization proposal was approved. According to the terms, with the exception of shares held by the founders and by shareholders who voted against the proposal, all issued common stock was to be bought and written off at the price of US$51.33 (equivalent to US$77 / ADS).

On April 19, Qihoo 360's privatization was approved by the National Development and Reform Commission (NDRC), with Tianjin Qixin Tongda Technology Ltd. listed as the legal person.

In May, Qihoo 360 agreed a plan with the State Administration of Foreign Exchange (SAFE) to exchange around US$7-7.5 billion.

Finally, on July 16, Qihoo 360 announced the completion of the

---

22 Including CITIC Guoan, Golden Brick Capital, Sequoia China, Taikang Life, Pingan Insurance, Sunshine Insurance, New China Capital, Huatai Ruilian and Huasheng Capital.

privatization process. It had taken more than a year, but as Zhou Hongyi had hoped, Qihoo 360 smoothly completed its privatization.

The focus shifted to how and when the company would re-list on the A-share market. The market had been speculating that it would do a backdoor listing, but on March 27, 2017, the official website of the CSRC's Tianjin Security Regulatory Commission revealed that Huatai United Securities had signed a listing advisory agreement with Qihoo 360, indicating that the company had taken on an IPO advisor. Nevertheless, there were still people who said that while queuing up for an IPO, Qihoo 360 was likely to do a backdoor listing.

Spin-off Listing

Besides its traditional businesses such as online search and security, Qihoo 360 sought new business opportunities in financing, smart phones and medical care. Given its significant scale, the markets also discussed whether or not Qihoo 360 would decide to undertake a spin-off for listing.

In fact, Zhou Hongyi began considering a new approach towards the capital markets early on and made the relevant arrangements. By the end of 2014, after establishing the joint-venture company Qiku in a US$400 million cooperation with Coolpad, he took the opportunity to adjust Qihoo 360's corporate structure, clarifying the division between its security business and new businesses (smart phones, smart hardware etc.). Qi Xiangdong was appointed as head of security, while Zhou Hongyi himself headed up the new businesses.

This adjustment was seen by the market as preparation by Qihoo 360 for spin-off listings that would see the company re-adjust its three core businesses – security, commercial (search, browser, distribution platform and other cash-flow products) and hardware – before seeking to list each separately.

The market saw several points in favor of such a spin-off listing strategy. First, the valuation models of traditional and new businesses are completely different, and bundling them together could impact listing valuations, while spin-off listings could allow each business to be valued based on comparative companies, improving the overall premium positioning of the company. Some analysts compared Qihoo 360's situation to that of Sohu, which allowed its portal, video and Sogou[23] businesses to develop and list separately. While there was a precedent in this regard, it was not universally seen as successful. Analysts argued that the era of "single combat" was over and that the trend to follow was the "group combat" approach championed by the BAT titans, working to build single-platform eco-systems to fend off challenges. Such an approach was more fault-tolerant, they said, and gave companies a greater opportunity to learn and improve.

Amidst rampant market speculation, in May 2015, Qihoo 360 stripped out its enterprise security business and formally set up an independent enterprise security group. When in July 2016, Qihoo 360 completed its privatization process, Zhou even said that, "Qihoo 360 will become a group, and I hope that in the next three to five years, there will be dozens to a hundred companies under the leadership of the 360 group, with several of them being listed." During the fifth China Internet Security Conference on September 12, 2017, the board chairman of the 360 Enterprise Security Group disclosed that, "360's security group isn't currently looking to be listed, we need to continue the fight for a few years before that." Based on this information, many now believe that Qihoo 360 will choose to list other business operations first, and seek a way to take the enterprise security group public separately.

Returning to the A-share Market

The market's guessing game on Qihoo 360's public offering ended on the morning of November 3, 2017 with a public announcement by SJEC Corporation[24] of its restructuring and listing plan. According to the statement, the two parties would engage in an asset swap worth RMB1.872 billion through asset replacement and cash transfers, and Qihoo 360 would take a 100 percent stake in the company, worth RMB50.416 billion. At the conclusion of the transactions, Qixinzhicheng, run by Zhou Hongyi, held 48.74% of the shares of the listed company.

The disclosure announcement indicated that the assets included in the backdoor listing were different from those held by the public company in the US. Apart from the absence of the Qihoo 360 corporate security business as planned, Zhou also stripped away non-cyber-security businesses including

---

23 Sogou search engine, Sogou input and Sogou browser.
24 A Shanghai-listed elevator manufacturer.

Qinfo Health, Qinfor Wealth, Qinfo Smart, Qinfo Oukong, Beijing LY and Qibu World, while only retaining Qihoo Tech, Qihoo 360 Tech, Qihoo Ceteng and other businesses involved with cyber security technology.

On February 28, 2018, 360 Security Technology Ltd. officially went public on the Shanghai Stock Exchange. On the first day of trading, its stock price rose by 3.84%, and its market value peaked at RMB444.2 billion, ranking it top among the A-share high-tech stocks. Compared to its market value of US$9.3 billion (RMB64.6 billion) when it left the U.S., Qihoo's value had gone up roughly sevenfold.

As the largest of China's Internet companies to re-list on the Chinese stock market through privatization, Qihoo 360's return attracted huge attention. At the listing ceremony, Zhou Hongyi said that Qihoo 360 would focus on three things. First, strengthening its core technologies and building on its original innovations, holding firm to the strategy of 'Security Comes First'. Second, innovating in big data and artificial intelligence. Third, leveraging its user base by greatly expanding content provision. "Many see a successful fundraise, a successful listing, as an end in itself, but for me, a listing is probably more of a starting point," Zhou said. "Regardless of whether it is a reboot or a refresh, it is a new start for 360."

This not only marked a new start for Qihoo 360, but also heralded a new era for the Chinese A-share market, in which it would support the "four new"[25] economic ecology by welcoming the domestic listing of "unicorns." On ringing Qihoo 360 in on the Shanghai Stock Exchange in February 2018, Zhou Hongyi declared, "360's return to the A share market will not be a special case. China has entered a new era, with its GDP ranked second in the world, and it needs a capital market to match. The reasons that led many Internet companies to list overseas are in the past. As technology continues to advance in China, 360 will just be the first of many high quality Internet companies on the A-share market."

---

25 These are: new technology, new industry, new environment, new models.

Professors'
Biographies

陈龙
Chen Long

Chief Strategy Officer of Ant Financial Services Group, Alibaba Group
Former Professor of Finance, CKGSB
PhD, University of Toronto

Areas of Expertise:
Applied Asset Pricing Theory,
Corporate Financing, Corporate
Strategy, Empirical Asset Pricing,
Futures Trading, Internet Finance

Chen Long is a former Professor of
Finance at Cheung Kong Graduate
School of Business (CKGSB). From
2001 to 2008, Dr. Chen served as
Assistant Professor of Finance at
Michigan State University, where he
received an Excellence in Teaching
Award in 2003. He has tenured at the
Olin School of Business at Washington
University. Dr. Chen now serves as the Chief
Strategy Officer of Ant Financial.

黄春燕
Huang Chunyan (Jennifer)

Professor of Finance, CKGSB
Academic Director for FMBA, CKGSB
PhD, Massachusetts Institute of Technology

Areas of Expertise:
Corporate Finance, Government Debt,
Internal Capital Allocation, Investment
Strategy, Liquidity and Asset Pricing,
Mutual Funds, Stock Market Crashes,
Taxes

Jennifer Huang is a Professor of
Finance at Cheung Kong Graduate
School of Business (CKGSB). She
previously tenured at the University
of Texas, Austin. Dr. Huang sits on
the editorial boards of Journal of
Pension Economics and Finance,
International Review of Applied
Financial Issues and Economics, and
International Review of Finance.

荆兵
Jing Bing

Associate Professor of Marketing, CKGSB
PhD, University of Rochester

Areas of Expertise:
E-Commerce, Product Customization, Product Differentiation,
Product Line Design and Pricing, Word of Mouth Marketing

Jing Bing is an Associate Professor of Marketing
at Cheung Kong Graduate School of Business
(CKGSB). Between 2001 and 2007, he was an
Assistant Professor of Information Systems
at the Stern School of Business at New York
University. Dr. Jing received the Outstanding
Researcher Award (Year 2011) at CKGSB.

李乐德
Li Lede (Lode)

Professor of Operations Management, CKGSB
Professor Emeritus at Yale University
PhD, Northwestern University

Areas of Expertise:
Game Theory, Management of International Manufacturing Networks, Operations Management and Strategy, Service Operations, Stochastic Process and Control, Supply Chain Management

Lode Li is a Professor of Operations Management at Cheung Kong Graduate School of Business (CKGSB). He previously taught at Yale University, the Massachusetts Institute of Technology, Northwestern University and Hong Kong University of Science and Technology. Dr. Li is on the editorial board of Management Science and Operation Research. His research has been regularly published in leading journals since 1985.

李伟
Li Wei

Professor of Economics, CKGSB
Director of CKGSB Case Center
Director of CKGSB China Economy and Sustainable Development Center
PhD, University of Michigan

Areas of Expertise:
Corruption, Financial Markets,
Macroeconomics, Managerial Incentives
and Market Competition, Real Estate,
Reform, Taxation, Telecommunications
Privatization, Valuation in Emerging
Markets

Li Wei is Professor of Economics at
Cheung Kong Graduate School of Business
(CKGSB). He formerly served as a professor
at the Darden Graduate School of Business,
University of Virginia. Previously, he was a
research associate at the University of Michigan's
Institute for Social Studies and taught at Duke
University's Fuqua School of Business.

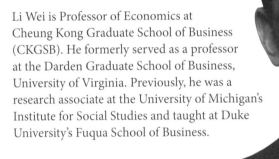

李洋
Li Yang

Associate Professor of Marketing, CKGSB
PhD, Columbia Business School

Areas of Expertise:
Big Data Methods, Bayesian
Nonparametrics, Machine Learning,
Choice Modeling, Pricing Strategy,
Retail Optimization, Social Networks

Li Yang is Associate Professor of
Marketing at Cheung Kong Graduate
School of Business (CKGSB).
Professor Li has published in
leading academic journals such as
Management Science, Marketing
Science, and Journal of Marketing
Research. He has also consulted for
Tencent, Baidu and Yonghui Groups, and
currently holds a US patent.

欧阳辉
Ou-Yang Hui

Dean's Distinguished Chair Professor of Finance, CKGSB
Associate Dean for MBA, CKGSB
Academic Director for EMBA, CKGSB
PhD, University of California, Berkeley
PhD, Tulane University

Areas of Expertise:
Asset Pricing, Corporate Finance, Fixed Income,
Integrated Models of Asset Pricing, Internet
Finance, Moral Hazard, Quantitative Strategies
and Research, Risk Management

Ou-Yang Hui is the Dean's Distinguished
Chair Professor of Finance at Cheung Kong
Graduate School of Business (CKGSB). He
previously served as an associate professor at
Duke University and an assistant professor
at UNC-Chapel Hill. Prof Ou-Yang was voted
the best teacher by Duke's Global EMBA Class
of 2004. He won the Barclays Global Investors/
Michael Brennan Runner-Up Award for the best
paper published in the Review of Financial Studies
in 2003 as well as the Best Paper Award (with
Professor Henry Cao) presented by the
Society of Quantitative Analysts in
2005. Before joining CKGSB,
Dr. Ou-Yang served as a
managing director at UBS
where he headed the
Quantitative Solutions/
Algo Strategies
division.

滕斌圣
Teng Bingsheng

Professor of Strategic Management
Associate Dean for CKGSB Asia and Europe
PhD, City University of New York

Areas of Expertise:
Chinese Firms' Global Strategies, Entrepreneurship and Innovation, M&A, Strategic Alliances, Strategic Management

Teng Bingsheng is Professor of Strategic Management at CKGSB and Associate Dean for CKGSB Asia and Europe. He formerly served as a tenured Professor of Strategic Management at George Washington University (GWU).

Teng has published over 20 articles in academic journals and his research is included in textbooks on strategic management. An authority on strategic alliances, he is regularly interviewed by international media.

Teng is a member of the Academy of Management and serves on the editorial board of International Entrepreneurship and Management Journal. He has received many awards for his research, and his biography appears in *Who's Who in America* and *Who's Who in American Higher Education*.

王砚波
Wang Yanbo

Assistant Professor, NUS Business School
Former Visiting Assistant Professor, CKGSB
PhD, Massachusetts Institute of Technology

Areas of Expertise:
Cooperation Strategies, Entrepreneurship, Financial
Fraud and China, Technology Innovation

Wang Yanbo was a former Visiting
Assistant Professor of Strategy and
Innovation at Cheung Kong Graduate
School of Business (CKGSB). Prior to
joining CKGSB, he was an Assistant
Professor of Strategy & Innovation at
Boston University Questrom School of
Management, as well as Visiting Scholar
to Stanford University Management
Science & Engineering (Summer 2010)
and Tsinghua University (January – June
2008). Dr. Wang is now working as the
Assistant Professor at NUS Business
School.

朱睿
Zhu Rui (Juliet)

Professor of Marketing, CKGSB
Co-director of the Branding Center, CKGSB
Associate Dean for EMBA Programs, CKGSB
PhD, University of Minnesota

Areas of Expertise:
Branding, Consumer Behavior, Consumer Information Processing and Psychology, Corporate Social Responsibility, Design and Structural Effects of Physical Environment, Innovative Business Models, Modern Philanthropy, Tencent

Zhu Rui is Professor of Marketing at Cheung Kong Graduate School of Business (CKGSB). Prior to joining CKGSB, she was Associate Professor of Marketing and Canada Research Chair in consumer behavior at the University of British Columbia. Professor Zhu has done extensive research on consumer behavior, creativity, and advertising. In 2015, Professor Zhu won the CKGSB Research Excellence Award. In 2010, Professor Zhu won the Sauder Research Excellence Award. In 2007, Professor Zhu won the Marketing Science Institute's Young Scholar award, which identified 20 scholars around the world who are leaders of the next generation of marketing academics. She was an American Marketing Association Sheth Foundation Doctoral Consortium Fellow in 2002.

Case Center Introduction

Founded in 2003, the CKGSB Case Center is committed to conducting research and producing business case studies. Our case studies showcase the transition and practices of a wide range of businesses in China, and our portfolio has become one of the school's vital knowledge assets.

With more than 400 published cases, we are proud that each one is based on a deep understanding of the China market and executed according to rigorous research standards. Each case study is lead by a CKGSB professor. The Case Center itself is directed by CKGSB Professor of Economics Li Wei, an acclaimed macroeconomics faculty member.

Our research spans various areas of the Chinese market: strategy, management, globalization, economics, marketing, operations, finance and accounting. Companies of different sizes are featured, as are a wealth of industries. Together, they represent the achievements and lessons learned of industry leaders. For example, in the field of technology innovation, the Case Center's cases on Baidu, Alibaba and Tencent illustrate how these three giants vie for the top position in today's mobile Internet era. On the subject of finance and capital markets, cases on Chinese companies, like Qihoo 360, that delisted from the US capital market to then relist in China, provide a new look at how companies are being financed. Other topics on unique Chinese business practices, such as Chinese family business succession and digital branding evolution, are also addressed in selected case studies.

CKGSB's cases serve as teaching material for our programs and as business insights for our wider audience. Caixin, Caijing, Financial Times and HBR, among numerous other top-tier global media, have all published our work. The Case Center has also published several books, most recently on how Chinese companies have leveraged the Internet to transform and upgrade their business models and on the dynamics and innovation of the Chinese finance sector.

For more information, please visit *http://*_____

Cheung Kong Graduate School of Business

Cheung Kong Graduate School of Business (CKGSB) aims to cultivate business leaders with a global vision, a humanistic spirit, a strong sense of social responsibility and an innovative mind-set. Established in Beijing in November 2002 with generous support from the Li Ka Shing Foundation, CKGSB is China's first faculty-governed, non-profit, independent business school.

Since its founding, CKGSB has developed into a prominent business school that stands apart for its cutting-edge China insights and its focus on technology disruptions that are socially desirable. Today, CKGSB has more than 40 full-time professors, many of whom previously held tenured faculty positions at leading business schools such as Wharton and Yale. Their research has provided the basis for more than 400 case studies of both China-specific and global issues. CKGSB also stands apart for its unmatched alumni network. More than half of CKGSB's 13,000 alumni are at the CEO or Chairman level and, collectively, they lead one fifth of China's most valuable brands.

CKGSB goes beyond the traditional boundaries of business schools to provide students with a more well-rounded understanding of business and to contribute to global social innovation. For instance, in 2005, CKGSB pioneered the integration of the humanities into its curricula to give students a long-term and holistic view of business and development. Moreover, all of the school's degree students are required to conduct community work before graduating. For instance, even the school's EMBA students—more than 80% of who are above the Vice President level—must complete six days of community service before receiving their degrees. In 2014, CKGSB was the first Chinese business school to develop a philanthropy program aimed at equipping the school's alumni with expertise on setting up and managing foundations, as well as engaging in social development.

CKGSB is also one of mainland China's most globalized business schools. Besides its three campuses in Beijing, Shanghai and Shenzhen, the school also has offices in London, New York and Hong Kong. Moreover, it has formed strategic partnerships for joint programs and research with more than 40 leading institutions worldwide, such as Berkeley Engineering and Columbia Engineering in the US, Churchill College at the University of Cambridge in the UK, and FDC in Brazil, among many others.

The school offers the following innovative courses: MBA, Part-time MBA, Executive MBA, Business Scholars Program; and Executive Education programs in several languages.

For more information, please visit *http://english.ckgsb.edu.cn/*.